Picasso at the Lapin Agile

and Other Plays

Picasso at the Lapin Agile and Other Plays

Picasso at the Lapin Agile

The Zig-Zag Woman

Patter for the Floating Lady

WASP

Steve Martin

Grove Press
New York

Copyright © 1996 by 40 Share Productions, Inc.

All rights reserved. No part of this book may be reproduced in any form or by any electronic or mechanical means, including information storage and retrieval systems, without permission in writing from the publisher, except by a reviewer, who may quote brief passages in a review. Any members of educational institutions wishing to photocopy part or all of the work for classroom use, or publishers who would like to obtain permission to include the work in an anthology, should send their inquiries to Grove/Atlantic, Inc., 841 Broadway, New York, NY 10003.

CAUTION: Professionals and amateurs are hereby warned that *Picasso at the Lapin Agile, The Zig-Zag Woman, Patter for the Floating Lady,* and *WASP* are subject to royalties. They are fully protected under the copyright laws of the United States, Canada, United Kingdom, and all British Commonwealth countries, and all countries covered by the International Copyright Union, the Pan-American Copyright Convention, and the Universal Copyright Convention. All rights, including professional, amateur, motion picture, recitation, public reading, radio broadcasting, television, video or sound taping, all other forms of mechanical or electronic reproduction, such as information storage and retrieval systems and photocopying, and rights of translation into foreign languages, are strictly reserved.

First-class professional, stock, and amateur applications for permission to perform them, and those other rights stated above, must be made in advance, before rehearsals begin, to International Creative Management, Inc., 40 West 57th Street, New York, New York 10019, Attention: Sam Cohn.

Published simultaneously in Canada
Printed in the United States of America

Library of Congress Cataloging-in-Publication Data

Martin, Steven, 1945–
    Picasso at the Lapin Agile and other plays / Steve Martin.
        p.   cm.
    1. Picasso, Pablo, 1881–1973—Drama. 2. Einstein, Albert,
1879–1955—Drama. 3. Artists—France—Paris—Drama. 4. Physicists—
France—Paris—Drama.   I. Title.
PS3563.A7293P53   1996
812'.54—dc20   96-13222

    ISBN 0-8021-3523-4 (pbk.)

Design by Laura Hammond Hough

Grove Press
841 Broadway
New York, NY 10003

02 10 9 8

Contents

Picasso at the Lapin Agile

Picasso at the Lapin Agile was first produced at the Steppenwolf
Theater Company in Chicago, with the following cast:

Freddy: *Tracy Letts*
Gaston: *Nathan Davis*
Germaine: *Rondi Reed*
Albert Einstein: *Jeff Perry*
Suzanne, Trishla, Female Admirer: *Paula Korologos*
Sagot: *Robert Breuler*
Pablo Picasso: *Tim Hopper*
Charles Dabernow Schmendiman: *Troy West*
A Visitor: *Travis Morris*

Director: *Randall Arney*
Scenic Designer: *Scott Bradley*
Lighting Designer: *Kevin Rigdon*
Costume Designer: *Allison Reeds*
Sound Designer: *Richard Woodbury*
Production Stage Manager: *Laura Koch*

Picasso at the Lapin Agile was produced on the New York
stage by Stephen Eich and Joan Stein, with the following cast:

Freddy: *Harry Groener*
Gaston: *Carl Don*
Germaine: *Rondi Reed*
Albert Einstein: *Mark Nelson*
Suzanne, Countess, Female Admirer: *Susan Floyd*
Sagot: *John Christopher Jones*
Pablo Picasso: *Tim Hopper*
Charles Dabernow Schmendiman: *Peter Jacobson*
A Visitor: *Gabriel Macht*

Director: *Randall Arney*
Scenic Designer: *Scott Bradley*
Lighting Designer: *Kevin Rigdon*
Costume Designer: *Patricia Zipprodt*

A bar in Paris, 1904. One year later, Albert Einstein published the special theory of relativity. Three years later, Pablo Picasso painted Les Demoiselles d'Avignon.

Cast in Order of Appearance:
Freddy, the owner and bartender of the Lapin Agile
Gaston, an older man
Germaine, waitress and Freddy's girlfriend
Albert Einstein, age twenty-five
Suzanne, nineteen
Sagot, Picasso's art dealer
Pablo Picasso, age twenty-three
Charles Dabernow Schmendiman, a young man
The Countess
A female admirer
A visitor

A bar in Paris, the Lapin Agile, circa 1904. A bartender, FREDDY, *rubs a rag across the bar. On the wall is a three-by-four-foot painting of sheep in a landscape. Upstage left is a door from the street. Upstage right is a door to a hall and toilet. We hear prerecorded accordion music of "Ta Rah Rah Boom Dee Re."* FREDDY *is taking chairs off the tables.*

GASTON (*singing offstage*): Ta ra ra *boom* dee re, ta rah rah *boom* dee re, ta rah rah *boom* dee re, ta rah rah *boom* dee re.

FREDDY (*looks up, rhapsodic*): There's something in the air tonight. (*Pause,* FREDDY *sneezes.*)

(*A man about sixty,* GASTON, *enters.*)

GASTON (*singing*): Ta rah rah *boom* dee re, ta rah rah *boom* dee re, ta rah rah *boom* dee re, ta rah rah *boom* dee re.

FREDDY: Well, Gaston, you sound like you're out of your bad mood.

GASTON: Yes, damn it. Woke up this morning, good mood. Nothing I could do about it. Ta rah rah *boom* dee re, ta rah rah *boom* dee re . . . Damn my memory, what's the next lyric?

FREDDY: I don't know, but my guess is it's "Ta rah rah *boom* dee re."

GASTON: Great song. I wonder who wrote it?

FREDDY: Two East Indian guys. Ta Rah and Rah Boom Dee Re.

GASTON (*sits*): I have to pee.

FREDDY: Already? You haven't had a drink yet.

GASTON: One day you'll understand.
  (GASTON *gets up, moves toward the toilet. Through the door,*
  EINSTEIN, *age twenty-five, enters, hair slicked and neat looking.*
  EINSTEIN *prepares to speak to* FREDDY. GASTON *starts to go to
  the toilet, then stops.*)

EINSTEIN: I'll be sitting there. I'm to meet a woman.

GASTON (*to* EINSTEIN): Oh, shut your face, you little pip-squeak!

FREDDY (*to* GASTON): Hey! You don't even know him.

GASTON: I have a feeling.

FREDDY: Still, you can't just insult someone right out of the blue.

GASTON: But I'm French.
  (GASTON *exits.*)

EINSTEIN: Do you have absinthe?

FREDDY: One absinthe coming up.

EINSTEIN: I'm supposed to meet her at six o'clock at the Bar Rouge.

FREDDY: This is not the Bar Rouge. It's the Lapin Agile.

EINSTEIN: No difference.

FREDDY: No difference?

EINSTEIN: You see, I'm a theorist, and the way I see it is that there is just as much chance of her wandering in here accidentally as there is of her wandering into the Bar Rouge on purpose. So where I wait for her is of no importance. It is of no importance where I tell her I will be. And the least of all, it's not important what time I am to meet her.

FREDDY: Unless . . .

EINSTEIN: Unless what?

FREDDY: Unless you really want to meet her.

EINSTEIN: I don't follow.

FREDDY: If you really want to meet her, you'll go to the Bar Rouge at the time you told her.

EINSTEIN: You're forgetting one thing.

FREDDY: What's that?

EINSTEIN: She thinks like I do.

FREDDY: Here's your vodka.

EINSTEIN: I asked for absinthe.

FREDDY: No difference.
       (EINSTEIN *takes the drink and sits down.* GASTON *reenters.*)

GASTON: I can describe the woman you're waiting for.

EINSTEIN: So can I!

GASTON: But I've never seen her. I can describe her hair, her clothes, her smell even.

EINSTEIN: Go ahead.

GASTON: But I need something.

EINSTEIN: Like what?

GASTON: Women are my area of expertise. And like the paleontologist, I can reconstruct the creature from a bone. But I need a hint.

EINSTEIN: How did you get to be such an expert?

GASTON: By looking.

EINSTEIN: So you're an admirer of the feminine equation?

GASTON: Yes, but I never touch. It's my saving grace. In that way, I glide among them, invisible. So I need a hint.

EINSTEIN: Yes, a hint. She has long red hair.

GASTON: Ah. One of those. Hard to control because she's so damn pert. She runs you, doesn't she? Her speech will be short, like her skirt. She'll sit over there and cross her legs and control the room. She's controlling it now. Look at us, talking about her, all because she has long red hair.

EINSTEIN: Sounds like you really know women.

GASTON: Never met one really.

EINSTEIN: Never met one?

GASTON: Not in my new incarnation as an older man. Women respond differently to men of different ages. I'm only newly old. Just getting used to it really. My name is Gaston.

EINSTEIN: My name is Albert Einstein.
(FREDDY *looks up suddenly.*)

FREDDY: You can't be. You just can't be.
(FREDDY *crosses from behind the bar and approaches* EINSTEIN.)

EINSTEIN: Sorry, I'm not myself today. (*He fluffs his hair, making himself look like Einstein.*) Better?

FREDDY: No, no, that's not what I mean. In order of appearance.

EINSTEIN: Come again?

FREDDY: In order of appearance. You're not third. (*Taking playbill from audience member.*) You're fourth. It says so right here: Cast in order of appearance. I knew you were fourth. I knew it when you walked in.

EINSTEIN: And yet you said nothing?

FREDDY: I couldn't put my finger on it. But now I can.
(FREDDY *gives back the program.*)

EINSTEIN: I take your point. Toilets!

GASTON: Behind that door.

EINSTEIN: Thank you.
>(EINSTEIN *exits. The waitress,* GERMAINE, *thirty-five, enters. She is Freddy's girlfriend.*)

GERMAINE: Sorry I'm late.

GASTON: You're not late; you're third.
>(GERMAINE *walks behind the bar, pours herself a drink, and swallows it.*)

FREDDY: Where were you?

GERMAINE: At home, darling.

FREDDY: Doing what?

GERMAINE: Sitting in front of a mirror.

FREDDY: Why?

GERMAINE: Just looking. Seeing what all the fuss is about. Besides, a mirror is like a mind: if you don't use it, it loses the power to reflect.

FREDDY: Well, you should try and be on time, sweetheart.

GERMAINE: Oh, don't be so old fashioned—these are the Naughts.

FREDDY: This is the fourth day you're late.

GERMAINE: Are we going to fight? Let's not fight, Freddy. Let's be in love like yesterday. (*She kisses him.*) So tomorrow I can say, "Let's be in love like yesterday." (*She kisses him again.*) Always. (*Another kiss.*) Always.

FREDDY (*breaks away*): Okay, always.

GERMAINE (*walks away*): I love you, even though you give me nothing.

FREDDY: What?

GERMAINE (*as in "oh, nothing"*): Nothing
(EINSTEIN *reenters, again from the street. He perfunctorily goes through his dialogue, panting.*)

EINSTEIN: I'll be sitting there. I am here to meet someone. A woman. I am to meet her at six o'clock. At the Bar Rouge. (*Then to* FREDDY:) All right?

GERMAINE: Bar Rouge? This is not the . . .

GASTON: Don't ask.

GERMAINE: Hey, Gaston. See any good ones today?

GASTON: Saw a good one yesterday as the shops were closing. I tried to hold her in my memory but she faded. All I remember now is a white linen blouse with just a whisper of brassiere underneath. It was like seeing a sweet custard through a veil of meringue.
(*An attractive nineteen-year-old girl,* SUZANNE, *comes through the door. She is street smart and in charge, and there're probably a few more broken hearts just from her walk to the Lapin Agile.*)

SUZANNE: I've heard Picasso comes here. (*Pause. They all look at her.*) Does he?

FREDDY: Sometimes.

SUZANNE: Tonight?

FREDDY: Maybe.
> (*This pleases her. She takes an article of clothing out of her bag. She turns her back to the audience and unbuttons her blouse, but before she takes it off, she stops and speaks first to* FREDDY.)

SUZANNE: Look away. (*Then to* EINSTEIN:) You look away too. (*She looks at* GASTON.) I guess you're okay. (*She takes off her blouse, revealing a black bra underneath, and puts on a new, sexier top.*) Okay.
> (*They all turn. She sits at a table and waits.*)

GASTON: Damn!

FREDDY: What's the matter?

GASTON: Now I have to consider everything I'm wearing today to be lucky. Every time I go out now, it's "not without my lucky hat, not without my lucky coat, not without my lucky shirt."

SUZANNE: I'd like some wine.

GERMAINE: Any special color?

SUZANNE: Red please.
> (GERMAINE *gets the wine from* FREDDY.)

GERMAINE: Do you know Picasso?

SUZANNE: Twice.

GERMAINE: Is he expecting you?

SUZANNE (*as in "of course"*): I think he's expecting to see me.

EINSTEIN: Who is this Picasso?

GERMAINE, FREDDY, AND SUZANNE: He's a painter . . .

FREDDY: He's a painter or says he's one. I've never seen his paintings, only what he says. Nuts about blue, they say.

SUZANNE: Oh yes, he's a painter. I've seen them. He gave me a
drawing.

FREDDY: What are they like?

SUZANNE: They're strange, really. (*She refers to the sheep painting
on the wall.*) Not like that, I'll tell you.

FREDDY: Nothing wrong with this picture. Got it out of my
grandmother's house just after she died; well, actually, while
she was dying. Sheep in a meadow in the fog. Beautiful.

EINSTEIN: That's not what I see.

FREDDY: And what do you see (*with pejorative emphasis*), *Einstein*?

EINSTEIN: I prefer to take it further. Observe how the sheep are
painted small, consumed by the weather and the terrain. So
I see "the power of the landscape over the small things." For
me, it's the meaning that gives it its value.

GASTON (*dismissive*): Jesus Christ! Sheep. Meadow. Fog. Period.

GERMAINE: There's a problem.

EINSTEIN: What?

GERMAINE: Well, it seems to me, if you judge it only by its mean-

ing, then any bad painting is just as good as any good painting if they have the same meaning.
(*There is a pause while everyone thinks.*)

EINSTEIN: Women!

GASTON: I would like a wine. The purpose of the wine is to get
me drunk. A bad wine will get me as drunk as a good wine.
I would like the good wine. And since the result is the same
no matter which wine I drink, I'd like to pay the bad wine
price. Is that where you're headed, Einstein?

FREDDY: I really don't think he's that clever, Gaston.

SUZANNE (*reaches in her bag and produces a folded-up piece of paper*):
Want to see the drawing he gave me?
(SUZANNE *hands it to* EINSTEIN. *He gets up, walks downstage
holding the drawing up, and examines it in the light.*)

EINSTEIN: I never thought the twentieth century would be handed
to me so casually . . . scratched out in pencil on a piece
of paper. Tools thousands of years old, waiting for someone to move them in just this way. I'm lucky tonight; I
was open to receive it. Another night and I might have
dismissed it with a joke or a cruel remark. Why didn't it
happen before, by accident? Why didn't Raphael doodle
this absentmindedly?

FREDDY: What do you think of the drawing?

EINSTEIN (*innocent*): What could it matter?

FREDDY: Huh? Let me see it. (*He looks at it.*) Hmmm. Yeah. Here.
(FREDDY *hands it to* GERMAINE.)

GERMAINE (*looks at it*): I like it all right.
   (GERMAINE *offers it to* GASTON, *who looks at it.*)

GASTON: I don't get it.

SUZANNE: I don't think it looks like me.

EINSTEIN: There you go. Four more opinions. I wonder how many opinions the world can hold. A billion? A trillion? Well, we've just added four. But look, the drawing stays the same.

FREDDY (*takes Einstein's glass to fill it*): Hey, look. What kind of a person would I be if I didn't form an opinion? I see the drawing, I think about it, I form an opinion. Then I see other people, and I express my opinion. Suddenly, I'm fascinating. (*He drinks Einstein's drink.*) And because I'm so fascinating, someone else sees the drawing, and they have an opinion, and they're fascinating too. Soon, whereas before I was standing in a room of dullards, I am now standing in a room of completely fascinating people with opinions.

SUZANNE: My name's Suzanne.

GASTON: And you're waiting for Picasso.

SUZANNE: Right. Do you know him?

GASTON: I've heard of him a bit. Big guy, rodeo rider, trick roper?

SUZANNE: Uh, no . . .

GASTON: What's his first name?

SUZANNE: Pablo.

GASTON: Oh no. Different guy. So how did you meet Pablo?

SUZANNE: I . . . it was about two weeks ago. I was walking down the street one afternoon and I turned up the stairs into my flat and I looked back and he was there, framed in the doorway, looking up at me. I couldn't see his face, because the light came in from behind him and he was in shadow, and he said, "I am Picasso." And I said, "Well, so what?" And then he said he wasn't sure yet, but he thinks that it means something in the future to be Picasso. He said that occasionally there is a Picasso, and he happens to be him. He said the twentieth century has to start somewhere and why not now. Then he said, "May I approach you," and I said, "Okay." He walked upstairs and picked up my wrist and turned it over and took his fingernail and scratched deeply on the back of my hand. In a second, in red, the image of a dove appeared. Then I thought, "Why is it that someone who wants me can hang around for months, and I even like him, but I'm not going to sleep with him; but someone else says the right thing and I'm on my back, not knowing what hit me?"

GERMAINE: Yeah, why is that?

FREDDY: Huh?

GERMAINE: Never mind.

SUZANNE: See, men are always talking about their things. Like it's not them.

GASTON: What things?

SUZANNE: The things between their legs.

GASTON: Ah, yes. Louie.

FREDDY AND EINSTEIN: Ah . . .

SUZANNE: See! It's not them; it's someone else. And it's true; it's like some rudderless firework snaking across town. But women have things too; they just work differently. They work from *up* here. (*She taps her head.*) So when the guy comes on to me through here, he's practically there already, done. So the next thing I know, he's inside the apartment and I said, "What do you want?" and he said he wanted my hair, he wanted my neck, my knees, my feet. He wanted his eyes on my eyes, his chest on my chest. He wanted the chairs in the room, the notepaper on the table; he wanted the paint from the walls. He wanted to consume me until there was nothing left. He said he wanted deliverance, and that I would be his savior. And he was speaking Spanish, which didn't hurt, I'll tell you. Well, at that point, the word *no* became like a Polish village: (*they look at her, waiting, then*) unpronounceable. (*Proudly.*) I held out for seconds! Frankly, I didn't enjoy it that much 'cause it was kinda quick.

GASTON: Premature ejaculation?

GERMAINE: Is there any other kind?

FREDDY: Huh?

GERMAINE: Never mind.

SUZANNE: So then, as I was sitting there half dressed, he picked up a drinking glass, of which I have two, and looked at me through the bottom. (*She picks up a glass and demonstrates.*) He kept pointing it at me and turning it in his hand like a kaleidoscope. And he said, "Even though you're refracted, you're still you." I didn't ask. Then he said he had to be somewhere, and I thought, "Sure," and he left.

GERMAINE: You saw him again?

SUZANNE: Oh yeah. That night he came back with this drawing and gave it to me, and we do it again. This time in French. I enjoyed it this time, if you're keeping score. Then he got very distracted and I said, "What's the matter?" and he said he sometimes starts thinking about something and can't stop. "Wait," he said, he doesn't think about it, he sees it. And I said, "What is it?" and he said, "It can't be named." That's exactly what he said: it can't be named. Well, when you're with someone who says they're seeing things that can't be named, you either want to run like hell or go with it. Well, I'm going with it, and that's why I'm here tonight. He told me about this place, that he might see me here one day, and that was two weeks ago.

GASTON: Sex, sex, sex.

SUZANNE: What?

GASTON: Oh, nothing, I was just thinking out loud.

SUZANNE: Been awhile?

GASTON: About eight months. Interesting, really. I saw a cat in the street and bent over to pet it, and it moved just out of my reach. It seemed friendly but nervous, so I followed it, always moving out of my reach. It must have been two feet out of my reach for several blocks, "Here, kitty, kitty, kitty," when I realized the cat had stopped at the feet of a woman. I looked up at her, and our eyes met. Older, my age, but she was dazzling. Let's just say she had a nice mortal coil. We made love in her place within the hour.

SUZANNE: Did you ever make love to her again?

GASTON: No, I didn't.

SUZANNE: See, there you are. She was there; you were taken with each other. You men; why is once enough? Why wouldn't you make love with her again?

GASTON: I would have, but she died about an hour later.

SUZANNE: Oh.

GASTON: We both wanted to do it again, and I told her I needed an hour to rejuvenate. I went outside and sat with the cat; and after a while, I looked up, and they were taking her body out on a stretcher.

SUZANNE: Oh, my God.

GASTON: I can't help but think that I killed her.
    (*Pause. Then* GASTON *emits a low, prideful chuckle.*)

FREDDY: What did Picasso say about my place?
    (FREDDY *starts sifting through some bills.*)

SUZANNE: He said this is where artists come to talk about . . . let's see . . . mana . . . mana . . .

EINSTEIN: Festos? Manifestos?

GERMAINE: Anyone want a coffee?

GASTON (*vehement*): That's what I could go for!

GERMAINE: Cream or black?

GASTON: No, a manifesto! I could really go for a nice, juicy manifesto. It would be nice to wake up and have a raison d'être

to go with your morning coffee, wouldn't you say? I have to pee.
(GASTON *goes to the loo.*)

EINSTEIN: Did Picasso say he was working on a manifesto?

SUZANNE: Oh no. He said he doesn't need one, and if he did come up with one, he would have exhausted it before he finished writing it down. Oh, one other thing. Just before he left, he went to the window and reached down on the sill and, like lightning, grabbed a pigeon. Then he held it in one hand and turned it upside down, and he soothed it and talked to it, and the pigeon fell asleep. Like it was hypnotized. Then he held his hand out the window and dropped the pigeon. And it just fell two stories upside down, straight down, like a stone. Then just seconds before it would have hit the ground, the pigeon turned itself over and started flapping like mad, and it took off flying, straight up past us, above the buildings and just away into the night. Then Picasso turned to me and said, "That's like me." And he was gone. Could I have a refill?
(GASTON *reenters.*)

GERMAINE: I'll get it. Anyone else want a refill?
(*Several respond.*)

FREDDY: Anybody know what 62 francs 33 minus 37 francs 17 is?

GERMAINE: Why don't you let me do that, Freddy?

EINSTEIN: Twenty-five francs sixteen.

FREDDY: You sure?

EINSTEIN: Twenty-five sixteen.

FREDDY: You're positive?

EINSTEIN: Positive. Absolutely.

FREDDY: It's just that you came up with it awfully quick.

EINSTEIN: Look, if you want it to be different, there's nothing I can do about it.

FREDDY: I'll work on it tomorrow.

EINSTEIN: It'll be the same tomorrow.

FREDDY: I've got my accountant friend coming over tomorrow; he can check it. He checks everything anyway.

EINSTEIN: You can have a math squad from the Vishnu Numerical Center for the Intellectually Profound come over, and it's still going to be 25 francs 16.

FREDDY: All right, all right.

GERMAINE: Jeez, Freddy. Take his word for it.

FREDDY: Are you a professor?

EINSTEIN: No, I'm not.

FREDDY: What do you do?

EINSTEIN: By day I work in the patent office.

GERMAINE: What do you do there?

EINSTEIN: By day I register notions. That's what they are really, notions. Shortcuts. How to get something to do something quicker.

GERMAINE: And what do you do at night?

EINSTEIN: Ah. At night . . . at night, the stars come out.

GERMAINE: The stars in the sky?

EINSTEIN: The stars in my head.

GERMAINE: And after the stars in your head come out?

EINSTEIN: I write it down.

FREDDY: Uh-huh. You been published?

EINSTEIN: No. No, not yet.

FREDDY: Yeah, well, we're all writers, aren't we? He's a writer that hasn't been published, and I'm a writer who hasn't written anything.
(FREDDY *goes back to his bills.*)

GERMAINE: And you're welcome here. We get a lot of artist types: writers, poets, painters. What do you write about?

EINSTEIN: I . . . I . . . I can't even begin to explain.

GERMAINE: Try. Simplify it. Can you say what it's about in one sentence?

EINSTEIN: It's about everything.

GERMAINE: You mean, like relationships between men and women?

EINSTEIN: Bigger.

GERMAINE: You mean, like life from birth to death?

EINSTEIN: Uh, bigger.

GERMAINE: Like the warring of nations and the movements of people?

EINSTEIN: Bigger.

GERMAINE: I see, sort of like the earth and its place in the solar system?

EINSTEIN: Keep going.

GERMAINE (*growing exasperated*): Okay. You're dealing with the universe and everything contained in it.

EINSTEIN: Why stop there?

GERMAINE (*giving up*): Okay. Okay. How big is this book?

EINSTEIN: About seventy pages.

GERMAINE: Hmm, not too long. That's good. Maybe we can put you in contact with some of our publisher friends. What's the title?

EINSTEIN: *The Special Theory of Relativity.*

FREDDY: Catchy.

GASTON: Judging from the title alone, I think it will sell at least as well as *The Critique of Pure Reason.*

GERMAINE: Is it funny?

EINSTEIN (*thinks*): Well . . .

GERMAINE: Because if it's funny, you can sell a lot of books.

EINSTEIN: It's very funny.

GERMAINE: Ah! It's very funny.

EINSTEIN: Well, actually, that depends on what you mean by "funny."

GERMAINE: Well, does it make you laugh?

EINSTEIN: No.

GERMAINE: Chuckle?

EINSTEIN: No.

GERMAINE: Smile?

EINSTEIN: I wish I could say yes.

GERMAINE: So it's not funny.

EINSTEIN: No.

GERMAINE: But you just said it was funny.

EINSTEIN: I was trying to sell more books.

GERMAINE (*exasperated*): Could it have illustrations?

EINSTEIN: Impossible.

GERMAINE: Why not? Might look good, give it some zip.

EINSTEIN: Illustrations are two dimensional.

GERMAINE: I know what you mean, but a good draftsman can give very realistic three-dimensional drawings.

EINSTEIN: I need four.

GERMAINE: Einstein, I'm trying to help you here. You want your book to have impact, don't you?

EINSTEIN: Sure.

GERMAINE: And if you want it to have impact, you've got to have people read it, don't you?

EINSTEIN: Yes . . .

GERMAINE: Okay, in your field, how many people do you figure have to read your book to have some impact?

EINSTEIN: One.

GERMAINE: No, no, no. In order for your book to have impact, you've got to have a lot of people read it; every man in the street has got to have one.

EINSTEIN: No, only one. Max.

GERMAINE: Max?

EINSTEIN: Max Planck, a German physicist, very influential. If he reads it, he makes my reputation.

GERMAINE: Well, you're lucky. If your market is one person and you know his name, you can put a limit on what you're going to spend on advertising. How old are you?

EINSTEIN: I'm twenty-five.

GASTON: You don't look twenty-five.

EINSTEIN: I discovered at an early age that I am the kind of person who will always look eighty-six.

FREDDY: Hey, Einstein, last week I bought twelve bottles of Chablis at seventeen francs a bottle, but only eleven came. How much do I owe this guy?

GERMAINE: Leave him alone.

EINSTEIN: One hundred eighty-seven francs.

FREDDY: See? As long as we've got him here, we might as will use him. I made a deal with Alphonse for a case of port at twenty-six francs each. He said if I bought six cases, he'd give me a discount of 2 to 4 percent. But he didn't know the year of the port. He said if the port arrived and was newer than 1900, he'd give me a 4 percent discount, keeping 3 percent on bottles before 1900 and 2 percent on bottles before 1895. When I got the cases, two cases had nine bottles dated after 1900 and fifteen bottles dated before 1895. One case had 18 percent of the bottles dated before 1900, and the rest were evenly split between before 1895 and after 1900. The rest of the three cases after 1900, before 1900, and before 1895 respectively. How much the hell do I owe this guy?

GERMAINE: Oh, good grief!

FREDDY: Oh, I left out one thing. He said if the sum total of the digits of the date of a bottle was greater than twenty-five he would give a 9 percent discount on those bottles.

EINSTEIN: Hmm.

FREDDY: He's stumped.

EINSTEIN: Oh, sorry, I wasn't listening. HA! Just kidding. Here's your answer: 2,245 francs 73 given that x end parenthesis y is the mean price per bottle.

FREDDY: Two thousand two hundred forty-five. Did you say, "Y end parenthesis x"?

EINSTEIN (*laughs heartily*): Y end parenthesis x? OH . . . THAT'S FUNNY!
(EINSTEIN *continues laughing. Pretty soon, they're all laughing, but they're not sure why.*)

FREDDY: What's the date today?

GERMAINE: It's the eighth.

FREDDY: And the year?

GERMAINE: You don't know the year?

FREDDY: I know the year . . . it's just that sometimes when you're writing fast, it's easy to write down the wrong year. Sometimes I look at a date I've written, and it's off by ten, sometimes fifteen years. But now that I'm thinking about it, I know it's 1903.

GERMAINE: '04.

FREDDY (*quickly*): '04. Okay . . . come on, the year just changed. It's only January.

GERMAINE: October.

FREDDY: The date isn't important anyway.

EINSTEIN: Just put "first decade of the twentieth century."

GERMAINE: Gosh, that's what it is, isn't it? The first decade of the twentieth century. I'm glad the nineteenth century is over. It was a bad century.

FREDDY: What's there not to like about a century?

GERMAINE: Well, for one thing, the pollution. Soot, garbage, smoke.

GASTON: Horseshit.

GERMAINE: You disagree?

GASTON: No, I'm adding to the list.

GERMAINE: Oh yeah . . . horseshit. Noise.

EINSTEIN: This century will be better.

FREDDY: What do you see for the future?

EINSTEIN: Let me ask you. What do you see?

GERMAINE: I'll answer. I see air travel becoming common, with hundreds of people being carried in giant airplanes. I think we'll see images sent through the air, and the receivers will become so popular that mass taste will diminish their potential. The city of Hiroshima will be completely modernized. (*Einstein's head jerks toward her.*) There will be a brief craze for lawn flamingos. Vast quantities of information will be stored in very small spaces. Cruelty will be perfected. By the end of the century, smoking in restaurants will be banned. (*They all react; how ludicrous.*) Music by four lads from Liverpool.

GASTON: Oh, brother.

FREDDY: Uh-huh.

SUZANNE (*dismissive*): Right.

EINSTEIN (*yeah, sure*): Next.

GERMAINE: Oh, well, fine.

SUZANNE: I think a yo-yo will be a wonderful thing to play with and a terrible thing to be.
(*The others look at her.*)

FREDDY: Here's mine. Led by Germany, this will be known as the century of peace. Clothes will be made of wax. There will be a craze for automobiles, but it will pass. The French will be the military might of Europe. Everyone will be doing a new dance called the Toad. A carton of cigarettes will be one of the most thoughtful get-well gifts. And the Wright brothers will be long remembered for the invention and manufacture of a low-calorie fudge . . .
(*Everyone nods: "Sounds about right . . . could be," etc.*)

(*A man enters. He is in his early fifties, a bit rotund, and nattily dressed. It is the art dealer* SAGOT, *vibrant and energetic. He goes over to* FREDDY.)

SAGOT: Anyone in tonight?

FREDDY: Not that you're looking for, Sagot.

SAGOT: I got a Matisse today, small but juicy. A little beachscape . . . give me a rum . . . I got him to give it to me. Here, take a look. (*He pulls out a small four-by-five-inch canvas and hands it to* FREDDY.) It says everything about Matisse you want to know. I bought eight drawings and got him to throw it in. The smaller it is, the harder it is to say it, no doubt about it, and that thing's got it all. This thing will hold a wall. Stick it up there.
(SAGOT *indicates the bar.* FREDDY *hands him a drink and puts the painting up on the back bar.* SAGOT *stands back.*)

SAGOT: Look at it . . . Beautiful (*he picks up* SUZANNE *and makes her look at the painting; he moves back a few more feet, stops*) . . . still works . . . (*a few more feet, stops*) . . . still working. Still holds the wall. (*He moves as far back as he can, stops.*) Lost it there. But, damn, you see what I mean?

SUZANNE: Not really.

SAGOT: Up to ten feet away, that bar is working for the Matisse. Then the bar takes over. (*He downs the rest of the drink.*) One more, Freddy.

GASTON: Does anyone feel a draft in here?

EINSTEIN (*indicates the Matisse*): What makes it so great?

SAGOT: I'll show you what makes it great. (*He goes to the bar and picks up the Matisse. He takes it out of its frame. He holds up the frame.*) This is what makes it great.

GASTON: The frame?

SAGOT: The boundaries. The edge. Otherwise, anything goes. You want to see a soccer game where the players can run up into the stands with the ball and order a beer? No. They've got to stay within the boundaries to make it interesting. In the right hands, this little space is as fertile as Eden.

EINSTEIN: That frame is about the size of my book.

SAGOT: Well, I hope you chose your words carefully. Ideas are like children: you have to watch over them, or they might go wrong.

FREDDY: I know what he means.

SAGOT (*to* EINSTEIN): I told that to Apollinaire; he squiggled and squirmed. (*To the Matisse:*) I'm going to turn a nice profit on that, you watch.

FREDDY: Well, considering you got it for free, it might not be too difficult.

EINSTEIN: But you got it because you loved it. How can you sell it?

SAGOT: What do you do?

EINSTEIN: I'm a physicist.

SAGOT: Good. Then you must know how naive a question can sound. I'll tell you how it works. (*He is drinking all the time through this.*) When I bought it, I identified it. I identified it as something worth having. I have named it as a work of art. Once I've done that, I don't have to own it. It will always be mine. And I guarantee you, Matisse is happy about it too. He wants his work out there, out of Paris. I've sold to Russia and I've sold to America and I've sold to dealers in Paris, who've sold everywhere. And the dealers like to buy from me because, frankly, they don't get it, and they want me to discern the good ones from the bad ones.

EINSTEIN: How did you learn to tell the difference?

SAGOT: I wish I knew! But I can look at two pictures that no one has ever seen before and know *that* one is for me (*points in the air*) and *that* one (*points to a different place*) is for the people whose idea of art is something ugly done by a relative. They come to the galleries with bags of money and say, "Show me what you've got; taste is no object!" (*He finishes his drink.*) Another, Freddy.

FREDDY: Finally, a customer.

SAGOT: Freddy, take out the book.

FREDDY: Come on . . .

SAGOT: No, take it out.
    (FREDDY *takes out a large book with engraved art plates. He opens the pages.* SAGOT *looks at the engravings only.*)

SAGOT: Courbet . . .(FREDDY *flips to another page.*) Courbet! . . . (*Another page.*) Courbet!

FREDDY: Wait a minute, this is a book about Courbet.
    (FREDDY *gets another book, opens the page, and shows it to* SAGOT.)

SAGOT: Titian! (*He takes a drink.* FREDDY *thumbs through the book and moves to a different plate.*) Raphael! (*He takes a drink;* FREDDY *shows another plate.*) Hmm, that's a tough one.

GASTON: You got the other ones, what's so tough about that one?

SAGOT: He's got his thumb over the name. (*He laughs big at his joke.*) We art dealers are notorious for our sense of humor!

FREDDY: All right. All right. That's enough.
  (SUZANNE *holds up the Picasso drawing and challenges* SAGOT. *He turns and sees it.* SAGOT *smiles.*)

SUZANNE: Who's this? (SAGOT *takes in the drawing.*)

SAGOT: Was he here this evening?

GERMAINE: Not yet.

SAGOT: Are you meeting him here?

SUZANNE: Don't know.

SAGOT: I can wait. (*He looks more closely at the drawing.*) A trifle hasty. Do you want to sell it?

SUZANNE: Not for anything.

SAGOT: For fifty francs?

SUZANNE: It is mine *forever.*

SAGOT (*giving up*): Get him to sign it. It'll be worth more.
  (*He sits down.*)

GERMAINE (*indicating the painting on the wall*): Hey, Sagot, you're the expert, what do *you* see?

SAGOT (*taking a short look*): Oh that. I see a five-hundred-pound lemon.

FREDDY: What?

GASTON: I have to pee.
 (*He exits.*)

SAGOT: I know that there are two subjects in paintings that no one will buy. One is Jesus, and the other is sheep. Love Him as much as they want, no one really wants a painting of Jesus in the living room. You're having a few people over, having a few drinks, and there's Jesus over the sofa. Somehow it doesn't work. And not in the bedroom either, obviously. I mean, you want Jesus watching over you but not while you're in the missionary position. You could put Him in the kitchen maybe, but then that's sort of insulting to Jesus. Jesus, ham sandwich, Jesus, ham sandwich; I wouldn't like it and neither would He. Can't sell a male nude either, unless they're messengers. Why a messenger would want to be nude I don't know. You'd think they'd at least need a little pouch or something. In fact, if a nude man showed up at my door and I asked, "Who is it," and he said, "Messenger," I would damn well look and see if he has a pouch, and if he doesn't, I'm not answering the door. Sheep are the same, don't ask me why, can't sell 'em.
 (*He sits down.*)

GASTON (*reentering*): Here's what I don't get. A month goes by, every night no different than tonight. People come in, people go out. So why do all the nuts show up in one evening?

GERMAINE: Picasso's definitely coming in tonight.

SUZANNE: I hope he comes in.

FREDDY: Me too. He owes me a bar bill.

EINSTEIN: I'd like to meet him.

SAGOT: Maybe I could get a painting out of him.

GERMAINE: Well, we all have an interest in Picasso; let's give a little toast to him.

EINSTEIN: I'll do it: to . . . Pi—
(*They all raise their glasses. Through the door,* PICASSO *enters, age twenty-three. He looks a little like Rodin's sculpture* Balzac, *only quicker. He seems moody, brooding.*)

PICASSO: I have been thinking about sex all day. Can't get it out of my mind.

GASTON: I've been thinking about it for sixty-two years.

PICASSO: I did sixteen drawings today, two in pencil, the rest in ink. All women. What does *that* tell you? It tells me a painter has got to stay well fucked; otherwise, the mind drifts off the easel, out the window, and across the street to the grocer's daughter. (*To* EINSTEIN:) You were proposing a toast.

EINSTEIN: Oh yes, to . . . Picasso.

PICASSO: Hey, to him. I mean, did you talk about anything else besides me? Did the weather come up?

EINSTEIN: It was mostly about you.

PICASSO: God, I feel good! How lucky for you! To be talking about someone, and then in they come. Anyway, how do I look? Be honest. That spot! (*He points to the sheep painting.*) We've got to do something about it. (*To* SAGOT:) Why don't you come by tomorrow? I have something to show you. Something's afoot. The moment is coming; I can feel it.

GASTON: How do you draw something? It seems so impossible.

PICASSO: It's all in the wrist. And the wrist starts here.
(PICASSO *points to his noggin.*)

SAGOT: The last month's work has been spectacular. I sat in front of the last piece I got from you with some friends and explained it for two hours.

PICASSO: Did they get it?

SAGOT: Don't know. They left after the first hour. I can tell you that the last hour was lonely, hard work.

PICASSO: Forget it. That was piss, piss, I tell you. This is different already. There is nothing in my way anymore. If I can think it, I can draw it. I used to have an idea; then a month later, I would draw it. The idea was a month ahead of its execution. Now the idea is ahead of the pencil only by minutes. One day, they will be simultaneous. (*He stands up, to the room:*) Do you know what that's like? If you can think it, you can draw it? The feeling of clear, undiluted vision?

EINSTEIN: *I* have a vague idea.

PICASSO: Are you an artist?

EINSTEIN: No, I'm a scientist, but sometimes I feel like an artist.

PICASSO (*jazzy*): Well, multiply it by a thousand, and you know what it's like to be me. (*He notices* SUZANNE, *scrapes his foot on the floor like a bull.*) I don't believe we've had the pleasure . . .

SUZANNE: Well, *you* have.

PICASSO: My name's Picasso.

SUZANNE: How nice for you.

PICASSO (*picks up her hand, scratches on the back of it with his nail; she doesn't look at it*): Look at it.

SUZANNE: It's a dove. (*She takes out her drawing and walks over to* SAGOT.) How much?

SAGOT: Fifty francs. (*To* PICASSO:) That's a good price, isn't it?

PICASSO (*realizing*): Yes, that's fair.

SUZANNE: It's the price of fame I guess.
(SUZANNE *starts to leave, but stops on Picasso's next line.*)

PICASSO (*getting up and walking over to* SAGOT): How much for the drawing?

SAGOT: Whatever you want.
(PICASSO *reaches in his pocket for money but he has none. He finds a pencil and sketches some lines on a napkin, finishes, and hands it to* SAGOT.)

PICASSO: Fair?

SAGOT: Very fair; this one's signed.
(PICASSO *takes the original drawing and kneels before* SUZANNE, *offering it to her. She accepts it; he starts to go.*)

SUZANNE: Sign it.
(SAGOT *silently claps.* PICASSO *signs it.*)

SUZANNE: I would like another drink.
(*She sits.*)

PICASSO (*to the room*): And I would like . . . a motorcar! Can I do that, Sagot? Can I draw my way into a car? Can I draw a camera and you sell it and suddenly I can have a camera? Can I get anything I want by just drawing it?

GERMAINE (*to* SAGOT): Can he?

SAGOT: Not yet.

PICASSO: And don't worry, because I never would. And don't forget it.

SAGOT: Anyway, if you need a camera, I've got one.

PICASSO: Good. Wait a minute. You have a camera?

SAGOT: Yes. I have a camera.

PICASSO: How did you get the camera?

SAGOT: I bought it.

PICASSO: Well, I have one question. If I can't afford a camera, how can you afford a camera? How much are you selling my paintings for?

SAGOT: Twice what I pay for them.

PICASSO: TWICE? Twice! I'm so depressed.

FREDDY: Actually, that's not so bad. You should hear what I'm making on the drinks.

PICASSO: Now there's *two* words I can't stand: *twice* and *perky*. (*Suddenly.*) God, he's good. I hate him! (*He crouches, tightening his body and grimacing.*) I hate him! I . . . hate . . . (*straightens his body, turns, and points to the Matisse on the*

bar) HIM! Just when you're in the swing of things, someone has to come along and ruin it for you. Ain't it the truth?
(*He picks it up, looks at it.*) It's so NEW. I can't even be mad.
This is not painting; it's alchemy. Ouch! It's sizzling hot! (*He
sets down the Matisse.*) Take it from me, folks, the boy can
paint. What's he like?

SAGOT: What's he like? He's earnest; talented, obviously; nice to
be around . . .

PICASSO: Ugh.

SAGOT: Self-deprecating . . .

PICASSO: Good. It saves me the trouble. (*He parks himself against
the bar; then, seeing the sheep painting on the wall:*) See, Sagot,
here's the difference between you and me. You look at that
nasty old thing and see a picture of some sheep in a landscape.

GASTON: He's not the only one.

PICASSO: Right! He's not the only one. Enter . . . me! I see it differently. I see it as an empty frame with something hideous
in it that's waiting to be filled up with something new. (*He
picks up a pencil and holds it like a foil.*) Advancing out into
the unknown, the undrawn, the new thing must be coaxed
out of its cave, wrestled with, and finally pinned up on the
wall like a hide. When I look at Goya, it's like he is reaching
his hand through the centuries to tap me on the shoulder.
When I paint, I feel like I am reaching my hand forward
hundreds of years to touch someone too.

GASTON: So it's like a relay.
(PICASSO *goes over to* SUZANNE, *picks her up, and starts dancing with her, no music. She's reluctant at first. They dance for
a while.*)

EINSTEIN: I work the same way. I make beautiful things with a pencil.

PICASSO: You? You're just a scientist! For me, the shortest distance between two points is *not* a straight line!

EINSTEIN: Likewise.

PICASSO (*still dancing*): Let's see one of your creations.
> (EINSTEIN *pulls out a pencil.* PICASSO *stops dancing, gets a pencil. The others back away as if it were a Western shoot-out.*)

PICASSO: Draw!
> (*They start to draw on the napkins.* EINSTEIN *finishes first.*)

EINSTEIN: Done!
> (EINSTEIN *and* PICASSO *swap drawings.*)

EINSTEIN: It's perfect.

PICASSO: Thank you.

EINSTEIN: I'm talking about mine.

PICASSO (*studies it*): It's a formula.

EINSTEIN: So's yours.

PICASSO: It *was* a little hastily drawn . . . yours is letters.

EINSTEIN: Yours is lines.

PICASSO: My lines mean something.

EINSTEIN: So do mine.

PICASSO: Mine is beautiful.

EINSTEIN (*indicates his own drawing*): Men have swooned on seeing that.

PICASSO: Mine touches the heart.

EINSTEIN: Mine touches the head.

PICASSO: Mine will change the future.

EINSTEIN (*holds his drawing*): Oh, and mine won't?
   (*Sensing victory, or at least parity,* EINSTEIN *starts to dance with* SUZANNE. PICASSO *stands befuddled.*)

PICASSO: Maybe you're a fake.

EINSTEIN: And maybe you're an *idiot savant*. And hold the *savant*.
   (EINSTEIN *continues dancing.* GASTON *watches.*)

GASTON (*suddenly singing*): WHEN A MAN, LOVES A WOMAN . . .

FREDDY: What the hell was that?

GASTON: I don't know; it just came over me.
   (SAGOT *gets out of his chair and starts to exit.*)

FREDDY: Where're ya going?

SAGOT: I'm going to get my camera. A night like this must be preserved on film. (*Referring to the painting on the wall.*) Picasso, do something about that ovine pastorale, will you?

PICASSO: The idea is coming.

SAGOT: I like it; sounds good.
    (SAGOT *exits.*)

PICASSO: The idea is coming. THE idea is coming.
    (EINSTEIN *dances* SUZANNE *to her seat. He signs his drawing and gives it to her.*)

FREDDY: Hey, tell me if you get this joke: A man goes into a bakery and says, "Can you mail a pie?" The baker says, "Yeah, I think we could." Then the man says, "Well, could you bake me a pie in the shape of the letter E?" And the baker says, "Yeah, I think we could do that. Come back tomorrow, and we'll have it for you." So the man comes back the next day, and the baker shows him the pie. The man says, "You idiot! That's a big E. I wanted a small e, a small e." So the baker says, "No problem, come back tomorrow, and I'll see what I can do." So the man comes back the next day, and the baker shows him the pie. The man says, "Perfect . . . it's perfect." Then the baker says, "So where do you want me to send it?" And the man says, "You know what . . . I think I'll eat it here." (*The others all stare at him. No laughs.*)

FREDDY: Guy told me that the other day; I didn't get it.

GERMAINE: It's surreal.

FREDDY: I guess that's why I didn't get it. I'm a symbolist.

GERMAINE: And a good-for-nothing one at that.

FREDDY: You calling me a good-for-nothing symbolist?

SUZANNE: What's symbolism?

GERMAINE: So far, it's a fancy excuse for not doing the dishes.

FREDDY: That's not fair. Your post-romanticism has gotten us into a lot of hot water around here.

GERMAINE: My romanticism is not *post*!

FREDDY: It most certainly is!

GERMAINE: It's *neo*.

FREDDY: Post!

GERMAINE: Neo!

FREDDY: Post!

GASTON: STOP IT BOTH OF YOU! My God! This is not some sleazy dive somewhere.

EINSTEIN: The reason the joke is funny is because of the perfect selection of the letter E. It couldn't be a A-shaped pie, because a is functioning as both article and noun—who needs it? It can't be a B-shaped pie because of the confusion of the letter B with the insect. And not a C-shaped pie either, because he would have never known it was a capital C, because C in uppercase and lowercase are the same pie. I'll come back to D. An F-shaped pie is just plain not funny. An H-shaped pie would be unstable: two vertical bars supported by a weaker crossing structure. An I-shaped pie is no good because of the dot problem: do you connect the dot to the pie, in which case it's not an I, or do you keep it separate, which raises the question, Is it a dot or is it a cupcake? A K-shaped pie has Kafka written all over it. An M-shaped pie doesn't work because of the M-W dilemma. M to whom? And need I mention sigma? An O-shaped pie doesn't work because a pie *is* O-shaped. A P-shaped pie doesn't work because the phrase "*P*-shaped pie" has this naughty calypso rhythm!

GASTON: Excuse me. You're not going to go through the entire alphabet are you, because I may only have a few good years left.

EINSTEIN: Of course not. Some of them are so obvious they needn't be mentioned. Like *Q* for example.
(*Big pause while everyone thinks.*)

GERMAINE: All right, what's the matter with *Q*?

EINSTEIN: Well a *Q* is just an *O* with a comma through it, and a comma-shaped pie is just a croissant.

GERMAINE: Thank you.

SUZANNE: You said you would come back to *D*.

GASTON: NO! I have to *L* . . . I mean, pee.
(GASTON *exits to the bathroom.*)

FREDDY: Wait a minute, you said the joke was funny. But it wasn't funny.

EINSTEIN: Oh yes it was. I laughed.

GERMAINE: No, you didn't.

EINSTEIN: Not now, no. I'll laugh later. An ice-box laugh.

FREDDY: An ice-box laugh?

EINSTEIN: Yes. You don't laugh now, but an hour later, you're at home, standing in front of the ice box, and you laugh.

GASTON (*offstage*): *E*-shaped pie! Hahahahahaha.

EINSTEIN: See? He's just getting it now. Probably through a process of elimination. [*Author will be in the downstairs lobby when this joke is delivered.*] (*To* FREDDY:) When did you hear the joke?

FREDDY: A year and a half ago.

EINSTEIN: Maybe you already laughed at that joke but thought you were laughing at something else.

FREDDY: You mean, something else funny happened, and I laughed, but really, I was laughing at this joke, which I may have heard a year ago?

EINSTEIN: Right.

FREDDY: So I might still "owe" a laugh at the other funny thing that happened?

EINSTEIN: Or not. You may have only thought the other thing that happened was funny, but it really wasn't; so you don't owe a laugh.

FREDDY: So instead of laughing at the thing I thought was funny, I was laughing at the thing I didn't think was funny.

EINSTEIN: Exactly.

FREDDY: There's only one problem.

EINSTEIN: What?

FREDDY: The thing that you think that I think wasn't really funny was when the cat went running across the kitchen floor to leap through the cat door, but it was locked. Now there's no way that wasn't funny.

PICASSO: How about you, my dear? What do you say?

SUZANNE: I've had my example of a bad joke.

PICASSO (*sits*): Oh, come on.

SUZANNE: You're a womanizing, bastard fraud.

PICASSO: If you're trying to praise me, that's a poor choice of words.

SUZANNE: You're ridiculous.

PICASSO: Look, I meant everything I said that night. I just forgot who I said it to. Stranger things will happen in your young life, believe me. Worse things.

SUZANNE: I believed you.

PICASSO: I believed it too. And now that I see you tonight, my dear, I'm believing it all over again. I remember a blue-green bed with a rose-colored spread over it. A tin half-moon on the wall, holding a candle. On your bedside table, there were three rings side by side with small turquoise stones, one with garnet, and next to them a pale pink ribbon. Later I picked it up off the floor. I can't remember your name.

SUZANNE: I never told it to you.

PICASSO: Yes, you did. I remember it now.

SUZANNE: I never told you.

PICASSO: Yes, you did, Suzanne.

SUZANNE: I don't remember.

PICASSO: My ear was inches from your mouth. You said your name to me, then spoke words half-whispered, words started and left unfinished, mixed with cries, passion obscuring their meaning. (*He leans in and kisses her.*) Do you remember?

SUZANNE: Yes.

PICASSO: I drew three pictures of you from memory.

SUZANNE: You did?

PICASSO: But I can do better.

SUZANNE: I'll be there later.

PICASSO: That's a coincidence. So will I.

SUZANNE: I should go now. (*She picks up her things.*) Good-bye, everyone. (*She goes over to* EINSTEIN.) Good-bye, Al. (*To* PICASSO:) When will you be there?

PICASSO: When the play's over.
    (SUZANNE *exits.*)

EINSTEIN: The cat door was locked!
    (GASTON *reenters from the bathroom.*)

GASTON: So who's the third?

FREDDY: What do you mean?

GASTON: Well, in this bar tonight are two men: one is Einstein; the other, Picasso. Both nearly the same age, who think that somehow their work is going to change the century. So let's give it to them, and say they are. One. Two. There must be a third; there's always a triptych: the Father, the Son, and the Holy Ghost; the three graces; not to mention that bad news always comes in threes. Need I say more?

EINSTEIN: So who is the third point in the triangle, so to speak?

GERMAINE: Maybe it's Matisse.

PICASSO: No! Matisse cannot be third! If he wants, he can be fourth or fifth, but he cannot be the third point in the triangle.

EINSTEIN: I hate to tell you this, but the idea of a triangle with four points will not fly. A triangle with four points is what Euclid rides into hell.

GERMAINE: Well, who is the third?
(*Enter* SCHMENDIMAN, *bursting in.*)

SCHMENDIMAN: You are lucky tonight. You were here at the moment, and you heard it straight from the horse's mouth. I will be changing the century. The other bars know it; you may as well, too.

EINSTEIN: And what is your name?

SCHMENDIMAN: Schmendiman. Charles Dabernow Schmendiman.

EINSTEIN: And how will you change the century?

SCHMENDIMAN: With my invention.

PICASSO: What is your invention?

SCHMENDIMAN: It's an inflexible and very brittle building material.

EINSTEIN: Oh? What's it made from?

SCHMENDIMAN: And I'll tell you what it's made from: equal parts of asbestos, kitten paws, and radium. The only problem with it is that building considerations only allow it to be used in Los Angeles, San Francisco, and the island of Krakatoa, east of Java. But still! That's a big market! So everyone have a drink! . . .

FREDDY: On you?

SCHMENDIMAN: Uh . . . no. Just have a drink and remember my name: Schmendiman.
(*The others say, "Schmendiman," rather lamely.*)

SCHMENDIMAN: You see there's a distinction between talent and genius. And it's not just that they are spelled completely different. Talent is the ability to say things well, but genius is the ability to, well, say things! Talent sells a million in a year, but genius sells five thousand a year for two hundred years! (*To* EINSTEIN:) Can you compute that, or am I movin' too fast for you? You have to work to have talent. But genius comes gift wrapped in a blue box from Tiffany's!

GASTON: Picasso, Einstein, and Schmendiman. Somehow it doesn't have a ring.

SCHMENDIMAN: Which one's Picasso? (GASTON *points.*) I've heard of you . . . nice work. If you like blue. Come to think of it, it's about time for a Spaniard again . . . I mean, it's been a long time since "Bell-ath-kweth" . . . I'm just needlin' ye! You would be interested in my process. Creation is easy! Just follow the path of least resistance. You're supposed to paint, butcha feel like dancin'? DANCE! You're supposed to write, butcha feel like singin'? SING! That's what I did.

Remember, the shortest distance between two points is a foot
and a half. No pun intended.

FREDDY: No pun achieved.

SCHMENDIMAN: I struggled to be a writer, but my heart told me to
invent a very britt le and inflexible building material, which
by the way is called Schmendimite. And I did! That's why
I know my place in history is secure . . . I followed my heart.
Next bar! (*He goes toward the door, saying like a cheer:*)
Schmenda . . . Schmenda . . . men men men! Wait! I just
had another idea! A tall pointy cap for dunces!
(SCHMENDIMAN *snaps his fingers. He exits.*)

GASTON: What the hell was that?

FREDDY: I admire his confidence. And nothing else.

EINSTEIN: Here's th e way I look at it. We're not so much going to
change the century as bend it. Let's say Picasso here is a
genius. The century is just flying along in space and it whiz-
zes by Picasso here and it picks up speed and it flings itself
off in a new direction. Like a comet veering left at the sun.
The century is just zig-zagging along, bending and curving,
influenced by the powerful gravity of people like Picasso.
But the century itself, because we're in it, appears to be
heading straight.

GASTON: How can something be curved but appear to be straight?
Come on, buddy.

EINSTEIN (*sarcastic*): Gee, I never thought of that. I guess you're
right. HOW ABOUT THE HORIZON, YOU NITWIT?

GASTON: Are you trying to get my goat?

EINSTEIN: No, I'm just trying to explain something. You'll be happy to know that not only is the horizon something that appears to be straight but is actually curved, but so is space in general.

GASTON: Horseshit.

EINSTEIN: Well, it just so happens that it is!

GASTON: Is not!

EINSTEIN: Is too!

GASTON: Is not!

EINSTEIN: Is too!

GASTON: Is not!

GERMAINE (*to* FREDDY): Neo.

FREDDY: Post!

GERMAINE: Neo!

FREDDY: Post!

PICASSO: Mine is not a formula!

EINSTEIN (*to* PICASSO): Is so!

FREDDY (*to* EINSTEIN): Is not!

EINSTEIN: Is so!

PICASSO (*to* FREDDY): Neo!

FREDDY: Post!

PICASSO: Neo!

EINSTEIN: Hold it! Not only is space curved, but light has mass, and it bends when it passes by large masses like the sun at a finite speed regardless of the motion of its source! (*He gasps.*) Uh-oh! (*To everyone:*) Oh, my God, I can't believe I just blurted out the ending of my book. What I just said is my business, and I hope it won't leave this room.

FREDDY: I'm glad you stopped me; I was just going to the phone.

GERMAINE: You want to hear a woman's opinion on this?

EINSTEIN: There is no woman's opinion. This is science.

GERMAINE: Are you saying women can't be scientists?

EINSTEIN: No! I'm saying there are no gender-related opinions on this matter. Madam Curie didn't say, "I think I've discovered radium; I better check with a man." No man's opinion, no woman's opinion. It's sexless.

GASTON: I know the feeling.

EINSTEIN: What I just said is the fundamental, end-all, final, not-subject-to-opinion absolute truth, depending on where you're standing.

FREDDY (*notices* PICASSO *thinking, hushes everyone*): Hey, Pablo, psst! Pabs . . . yo, Picasso! . . . Easel head! Hey, blue boy! What's with you?

PICASSO: Sorry, I was just trying not to have an idea.

EINSTEIN: You have a lot of ideas?

PICASSO: Endless.

GASTON: How do you draw something? It seems so impossible.

PICASSO: What do you mean?

GASTON: Well, you're a painter; you're always having to come up with ideas. What's it like? I mean, the only idea I ever came up with was when I had to paint my shutters. I had to figure out a color. And I thought about it for a long time. Should they be a light color or a dark color? For a while, forest blue seemed nice; then, I realized there was no such thing as forest blue. I tried to flip a coin but lost it on the roof. I started thinking, "What are shutters anyway, and what would their natural color be?" Then I realized that shutters don't occur in nature, so they don't have a natural color. Suddenly, I knew I was just moments away from a decision, just moments, finally. Then this gorgeous thing walks by, with ruby lips and a derriere the shape of a valentine. I swiveled my head around and snapped a tendon. That put the decision off for three days. Then I thought, "Maybe just take off the shutters"; I started to think about moving to a land where there are no shutters and, frankly, suicide. But then one day, I said to myself, "Green," and that was it.
(GASTON *exits to the bathroom.*)

PICASSO: My process is just like that, but leave out the start, all the middle parts, and jump to the end. If I asked myself what color I wanted, it would just slow me down.

FREDDY: I know what he means.
(FREDDY *splashes together a drink.*)

PICASSO: Well, I see other painters struggling with it, killing themselves over it even. And I don't get their worry. I put the
pencil to the paper, and it comes out. Not the craft, mind
you, that was difficult to get. The ideas are a different matter. The ideas swoop down on me, they fall like rain, they
land with a crash.

EINSTEIN: They "thunk," too.

PICASSO: Absolutely! They thunk.

EINSTEIN: You too?

PICASSO: Yes. And pop.

EINSTEIN: Well, pop all the time, that goes without saying. They
never seem to flow, though.

PICASSO: Never. Flowing is a myth.

EINSTEIN: Never flow. Well, sometimes.

PICASSO: Yeah, sometimes.

FREDDY: Where do they come from?

PICASSO: Before me, artists used to get ideas from the past. But as
of this moment, they are coming from the future, fast and
loose.

EINSTEIN: Absolutely from the future.

PICASSO: I think in the moment of pencil to paper, the future is
mapped out in the face of the person drawn. Imagine that
the pencil is pushed hard enough, and the lead goes through
the paper into another dimension.
(PICASSO *and* EINSTEIN *start to get excited.*)

EINSTEIN: Yes!

PICASSO: A kind of fourth dimension, if that's what you want to call it . . .

EINSTEIN: I can't believe you're saying this! A fourth dimension!

PICASSO: And that fourth dimension is . . . the future.

EINSTEIN: Wrong.

PICASSO (*arguing*): The pencil pokes into the future and sucks up ideas and transfers them to the paper, for Christ's sake. And what the hell do you know about it anyway . . . you're a scientist! You just want theories . . .

EINSTEIN: Yes, and like you, the theories must be beautiful. You know why the sun doesn't revolve around the earth? Because the idea is not beautiful enough. If you're trying to prove that the sun revolves around the earth, in order to make the theory fit the facts, you have to have the planets moving backwards, and the sun doing loop-the-loops. Too ugly. Way ugly.

PICASSO: So you're saying you bring a beautiful idea into being?

EINSTEIN: Yes. We create a system and see if the facts can fit it.

PICASSO: So you're not just describing the world as it is?

EINSTEIN: No! We are creating a new way of looking at the world!

PICASSO: So you're saying you dream the impossible and put it into effect?

EINSTEIN: Exactly.

PICASSO: Brother!

EINSTEIN: Brother!
(PICASSO *and* EINSTEIN *hug.*)

GERMAINE: Oh, please. You two are spouting a lot of bullshit, and I say, the only reason you got into physics and art in the first place is to meet girls.

PICASSO AND EINSTEIN: What?!!!

EINSTEIN: You actually think I said to myself, "How can I meet a lot of girls? I know, I'll develop a unified field theory"?

GERMAINE: Look, I'm not saying you're not sincere, but let's face it, (*to* EINSTEIN) you've got some splashy party talk, and (*to* PICASSO) you've got the perfect and oldest pick-up line: I'd like to draw you.

PICASSO: That's outrageous.

GERMAINE: Maybe it's unconscious. I just think that somewhere way back, you realized you weren't maybe the handsomest things around and decided to go a different route.

EINSTEIN: I'm disgusted!
(*A woman enters. She wears glasses; is brainy, well dressed; has long red hair.*)

EINSTEIN: Countess!

COUNTESS: Albert!

EINSTEIN: Did you go to the Bar Rouge?

COUNTESS: Of course not, that's where you said we'd meet.

EINSTEIN: Oh, how stupid of me. Of course, you'd come here.

COUNTESS: Now what was that you were saying about it being impossible to distinguish motion produced by an outside gravitational force?

EINSTEIN (*aside*): God, she's sexy! . . .
(EINSTEIN *and the* COUNTESS *start to leave.*)

EINSTEIN (*mumbles*): It's impossible to distinguish, you know, two bodies unified . . . in a field . . .
(*The* COUNTESS *pays.* EINSTEIN *is a little embarrassed but not enough to stop her.*)

EINSTEIN (*turns to the room, suddenly waxing rhapsodic*): Although we may never meet again, like the roots of the sequoia grabbing deep in the earth, the ideas we have said here tonight will lace themselves irrevocably through the century.

PICASSO (*full of himself*): This is the night the earth fell quiet and listened to a conversation!

EINSTEIN (*the same*): O Lapin Agile!

PICASSO: Picasso, Einstein, Picasso, Einstein. My only regret is that we'll be in different volumes in the encyclopedia.

EINSTEIN: But there'll be no Schmendiman to come between us.
(EINSTEIN *and the* COUNTESS *exit.*)

PICASSO: I envy him.

FREDDY: Why's that?

PICASSO: In science, there's no reason to ever get cynical.

FREDDY: Why would an artist get cynical?

PICASSO: I think it's called marketing.

FREDDY: I've got to run next door and catch Antoine before he leaves town without paying his bar tab. (*To audience:*) I might be gone a longer amount of time than you'd think it would take a person to run next door and catch Antoine before he leaves town without paying his bar tab, but traditionally, it's okay. (*And* FREDDY *exits.* GASTON *reenters.*)

PICASSO: Gaston, don't you have to pee?
(GASTON *realizes he does and exits.* PICASSO *walks over to* GERMAINE, *and they kiss; you can tell it's not the first time. They break.*)

PICASSO: Tasty. Quite tasty.

GERMAINE: What was I? Dessert?

PICASSO: What do you mean?

GERMAINE: I mean, how many meals have you had today?

PICASSO: Why be nasty? We're not so different . . .

GERMAINE: Oh yes, we slept together, but there's a difference. Women are your world. For me, you are the thing that never happened. You and Freddy exist in separate universes. What I do in one has nothing to do with the other.

PICASSO: How convenient.

GERMAINE: Oh, don't get me wrong. I'm not being nasty. I like you. It's just that I know about men like you.

PICASSO: Men like me? Where are there men like me?

GERMAINE: Have a drink. You don't want me to go on.

PICASSO: No, tell me about men like me.

GERMAINE (*settles in*): A steady woman is important to you because then you know for sure you have someone to go home to in case you can't find someone else. You notice every woman, don't you?

PICASSO: Many.

GERMAINE: I mean, every woman. Waitresses, wives, weavers, laundresses, ushers, actresses, women in wheelchairs. You notice them, don't you?

PICASSO: Yes.

GERMAINE: And when you see a woman, you think, "I wonder what she would be like." You could be bouncing your baby on your knee, and if a woman walks by, you wonder what she would be like.

PICASSO: Go on.

GERMAINE: You have two in one night when the lies work out, and you feel it's your right. The rules don't apply to you because the rules were made up by women, and they have to be if there's going to be any society at all. You cancel one when someone better comes along. They find you funny, bohemian, irresistible. You like them young, because you can bamboozle them, and they think you're great. You want them when *you* want them, never when they want you. Afterwards, you can't wait to leave, or if you're unlucky enough to have her at your place, you can't wait for *her* to leave, because the truth is, we don't exist afterwards, and all conversation becomes meaningless because it's not going to get you anywhere because it already got you there. You're unreachable. Your whole act is a camouflage. But you are lucky because you have a true talent that you are too wise to abuse. And because of that, you will always be desirable. So when you wear out one woman, there will be another who wants to taste it, who wants to be next to someone like you. So you'll never have to earn a woman, and you'll never appreciate one.

PICASSO: But I appreciate women. I draw them, don't I?

GERMAINE: Well, that's because we're so goddamn beautiful, isn't it?

PICASSO: Germaine, men want, and women are wanted. That's the way it is, and that's the way it will always be.

GERMAINE: That may be true, but why be greedy? By the way, I knew you were using me, but I was using you back.

PICASSO: How?

GERMAINE: Now I know what a painter is like, tomorrow night a street paver maybe or a newsagent or maybe a bookseller. A street paver may not have anything to talk about to a girl like me, but I can write my romantic scenarios in my head and pull them down like a screen in front of me to project my fantasies onto. Like you project your fantasies onto a piece of paper.

PICASSO: How does Freddy fit in? Why are you with him?

GERMAINE: *His* faults I can live with. And occasionally, occasionally, he says something so stunning I'm just glad to have been there. But really? What I wouldn't give for a country boy. (FREDDY *reenters*.)

FREDDY: Well, I caught the son of a bitch in time.

GERMAINE: Not quite.
(*A young* FEMALE ADMIRER *charges into the bar. She looks around.*)

FEMALE ADMIRER: I heard that he comes here. Is that true? I mean, is that really true? (*She notices* PICASSO.) OH, MY GOD! Oh, my God. You. May I approach? May I really approach? (*She walks toward him.*) I can't believe it. What is it like to be you? I mean, what is it really like? . . . (*As she looks into his face, her demeanor changes.*) Wait a minute, you're not Schmendiman!
(*Bored, the* FEMALE ADMIRER *walks toward the door, exits.*)

PICASSO: Well, another typical night.
(PICASSO *wanders over and stands staring at the painting. He becomes lost in it.* GASTON *reenters.*)

GASTON: I learned something here tonight.

FREDDY: What's that, Gaston?

GASTON: You take a couple of geniuses, put them in a room to-gether, and . . . wow.

FREDDY: Boy, you really know how to turn a phrase.

GASTON (*pridefully bowing*): Well, thank you!

FREDDY: I was being ironic.

GASTON: So was I. That's my own little genius.

FREDDY: I'm sorry I missed it.

GASTON: Sometimes genius comes from very strange quarters . . .
  (*Enter from the toilet door a* VISITOR, *a singer from the fifties,
  age twenty-five. He wears blue suede shoes and has jet black hair.
  He shakes stardust from his shoulders, looks around curiously.
  Everyone eyes him as he goes up to the bar, looks at the Matisse
  painting, wanders away, swivels his hips at* GASTON, *finds that
  funny, sits down.*)

GASTON: Don't tell me you're a genius too.

VISITOR: Shucks, no.

GERMAINE: Something to drink?

VISITOR: Sorry, ma'am, don't drink. Do you have a tomato juice?
  I'm just a country boy.
  (GERMAINE *collapses, then gets up.*)

FREDDY: Sure we do. You want something in that?

VISITOR: Like what?

FREDDY: Well, like vodka.

VISITOR (*giggles*): You're kiddin'.
  (GERMAINE *goes weak in the knees again, gets up.*)

VISITOR: By the way, watch the shoes.

FREDDY: What brings you here?

VISITOR: Well, I kinda like surprising people, you know, poppin' up
  where you're least expected, supermarkets, fairgrounds. One

thing I like to do is get in people's snapshots, so when they develop 'em, I'm in their picture. But I got a little bored, so I thought I'd do a little time travelin'. Try another time zone.

GASTON: Put some vodka in it.

VISITOR (*looks around at the group in the bar*): You seem like some pretty nice folks.

FREDDY (*offended*): Pretty nice folks? What the hell are pretty nice folks?

GERMAINE: Yeah. What are you talking about?

VISITOR: Well, you know, friendly, good natured. Accepting of strangers.

FREDDY: Why would I want to be that?

GASTON: Yeah, what the hell are you trying to imply?

VISITOR: Well, where I come from, that's what people are like.

GERMAINE: Where are you from?

VISITOR: Memphis.

FREDDY: Memphis, Egypt?

VISITOR: No sir. Memphis is in America.
    (*"Oh." Silence.* FREDDY *starts polishing the bar.* GERMAINE *starts cleaning glasses.* GASTON *takes a long swig.*)

GASTON: What's Hiawatha really like?
    (EINSTEIN *enters with the* COUNTESS, *tipsy.*)

EINSTEIN (*to the* COUNTESS): Apparently, the cat door was locked. (*He notices where he is.*) Oh, my God. We've ended up where we started from.

COUNTESS (*nudges* EINSTEIN): Not only is space curved, so is Paris! (*The* COUNTESS *laughs.*)

EINSTEIN (*to* VISITOR): I don't believe we've met.

VISITOR: Oh yes, we will.

EINSTEIN: You and I think alike.
(EINSTEIN *starts to move toward him.*)

VISITOR: Watch the shoes.

EINSTEIN (*halts*): What do you do?

VISITOR: Well, ah guess ah . . . (*thinks*) sing songs about love.
(*The others take a breath,* GERMAINE *especially.*)

FREDDY (*rhapsodic*): If only I could sing songs about love.

GERMAINE: If I could sing songs about love, I would sing and re-member lovers past, and the emotion would infuse itself into the lyric.

PICASSO: I would give it all up if I could sing songs about love. No more paints or brushes . . . just the moonlight, the June light, and you.

GASTON: In the summer evenings, I would stand along the Seine and just sing, sing, sing.

EINSTEIN: People crowding in a smoky cabaret to hear the song stylings of Albert Einstein . . . appearing nightly with the Kentuckymen. Singing songs as pretty as a summer dress . . . lover's hand going into lover's hand.

VISITOR: See what I mean, about you all being pretty nice folks?
(*They all are embarrassed.* SAGOT *enters, carrying a tripod camera.*)

SAGOT: Good. You're all still here.

PICASSO: That's the camera?

SAGOT: The latest.

PICASSO: They're making them so small! Where did you get it?

SAGOT: I bought it from a Japanese tourist. Okay, everybody group together over there.
(*They all start to primp.*)

EINSTEIN: I'd like to order three one-by-twos and a daguerreotype.

SAGOT: Come, everybody. In a row and squeeze together.
(*The others all assemble for the photo.*)

GERMAINE: I hate having my picture taken.

SAGOT (*to the* VISITOR, *who hangs out away from camera*): You get in there too.

VISITOR: Oh, don't worry. I'll be in it.

SAGOT: Who are you, by the way?
(SAGOT *buries his head under the camera cloth.*)

VISITOR: I guess you could say I'm a messenger.
(SAGOT *emerges from under the camera cloth and eyes the* VISITOR *up and down, then recovers.*)

SAGOT (*announces*): On this day in 1904, the Lapin Agile was the site of this historic photo.
(SCHMENDIMAN *enters.*)

SCHMENDIMAN: Did someone say, "Historic photo"? (*He takes out a compact, powders his nose, and kneels in front with his arms outstretched.*) Can you still see the others?

SAGOT: Sure can.

SCHMENDIMAN (*disappointed*): Oh.

SAGOT: Okay, everybody, smile.
(*Erratic smiling. Some do, some don't. It goes in and out. As some get the smile, others lose it.*)

SAGOT: Hold it. You're not all smiling.

EVERYBODY (*ad lib*): Well, it's difficult, it feels fake. Why? (*Etc.*)

SAGOT: Okay. Okay. How about this? We'll think up a word that makes the face go naturally into a smile, and we'll all say it at the same time.

EVERYBODY (*ad lib*): Yeah, okay . . . good idea.
(*They all think.*)

SAGOT: Hmm. What's the word . . . what's the word. I've got it. Matisse.
(SAGOT *says it a couple of times to check, and his mouth goes into a smile. All try as they reform in a group.*)

SAGOT (*gets behind the camera*): Okay, everyone, say "Matisse." One, two, three.
(*They all say it and smile, except* PICASSO, *who frowns.*)

SAGOT: Try again, one more time.
(*They say, "Matisse"; everyone smiles but* PICASSO.)

SAGOT: Picasso, you're not smiling!

PICASSO: Well, I just can't! Not if you're going to say "Matisse"!
(*They all think some more.*)

EINSTEIN: How about Rubens?

PICASSO: Oh, please.

SAGOT: How about Michelangelo Buonarroti?

GASTON: We haven't got time for everyone to say "Nicholangleo Canelloni"!

PICASSO: El Greco! We can say "El Greco."

GERMAINE: El Greco doesn't make our mouths go in a smile; it makes it go in an O. We'll all look like fish.
(*In unison, they try "El Grec-oh." They don't like it. They all think some more.*)

COUNTESS: I've got one. How about "twice"? (*Smiles as she says it.*)

PICASSO: No! Not "twice."

COUNTESS: "Perky"?
(*All shake their heads no. They all start to think again.*)

SCHMENDIMAN: How about "cheese"?
(*This stops them. They like it.*)

SAGOT: "Cheese" is good.

SCHMENDIMAN: Chalk up another one for me!

SAGOT: Okay, everybody, say "cheese."
(*They all say, "cheese," and the photo is taken. They are all blinded by the flash.*)

SAGOT: Did the flash go off?

VISITOR (*drinks the vodka and tomato juice*): A-well-a, bless-a my soul-a, what's-a wrong with me? Whew, that's strong stuff. (*Pause as the* VISITOR *looks at the painting of sheep in a landscape.*)

VISITOR: Boy, oh boy, what a weird paintin'.

GASTON: Weird? It's just sheep.

VISITOR: Sheep? Looks like five women to me.
(*Picasso's head snaps around to the picture.*)

VISITOR: You puttin' me on? You see sheep?

GASTON: I see sheep, she sees sheep. Everyone in here sees sheep except for you.

VISITOR: Well, mercy. It looks like five weird women to me.

PICASSO (*stopped*): Where did you say you were from?

VISITOR: From the future.

PICASSO: And why are you here?

VISITOR: She sent me with a message.

PICASSO: Who is *she*?

VISITOR: She is the one who whispers in your ear every time you touch the pencil to the paper.

PICASSO: And what is the message?

VISITOR: Are you open to receive it?

PICASSO: Yes.

VISITOR: You better stand back.
   (PICASSO *stands, thinks, then steps back. The* VISITOR *gestures toward the painting. The painting changes into the full-size, eight-foot-square painting of Picasso's* Les Demoiselles d'Avignon. PICASSO *and the* VISITOR *stare at the painting in wonder. No one else, of course, sees it.* PICASSO *turns away from the painting, entranced.*)

PICASSO (*to himself*): I could dream it forever and still not do it, but when the time comes for it to be done, God, I want to be ready for it, to be ready for the moment of convergence between the thing done and the doing of it, between the thing to be made and its maker. At that moment, I am speaking for everyone; I am dreaming for the billions yet to come; I am taking the part of us that cannot be understood by God, and letting it bleed from the wrist onto the canvas. And it can only be made, because I have felt these things: my lust, my greed, my hatred, my happiness. (*He turns to the bar.*) So this is what it's like.

GERMAINE: What?

PICASSO: To be there at the moment.

GASTON: What moment?

PICASSO: The moment I leave blue behind. I'd like some wine.

GERMAINE: Any special color?

PICASSO (*looks back at the painting*): Rosé.

PICASSO (*to the* VISITOR): My name is Picasso. Are you an artist?

VISITOR: I had my moment.

PICASSO: What kind of moment?

VISITOR: I had my moment of . . . perfection.

PICASSO: I know the feeling. I just had it over there.

VISITOR: It's a good feeling.

PICASSO: Yes, it is.

VISITOR: I think not many people have it.

PICASSO: No. No, they don't.

VISITOR: Hard to know when it's happening, till it's over.

PICASSO: Don't tell anyone that; better to let them think you always knew.

VISITOR: Yes sir.

PICASSO: Don't let anyone in on the fact that we can't help it. We're like the chickens that cross the road. We do it and we don't know why.

VISITOR: Yes sir.

PICASSO: And remember, in a sense, we are both exalted because we are originals.

VISITOR: Well, that's a pretty bold statement, Mr. Picasso, considering we both took ideas from the art of the Negro.
(*Magic music. The set pulls away, revealing a backdrop of stars
in the sky. The painting is still visible.* EINSTEIN *pops out of his
chair, looking up.*)

EINSTEIN: Did you see that?

VISITOR: The roof is gone.

EINSTEIN: The stars have come out.

PICASSO: Millions and millions of stars.

EINSTEIN: You're way low.

VISITOR: It's night. I didn't know it was night, you know, the time
traveling thing. I arrive, I don't know if it's lunch or dinner
or what. I've put on eighteen pounds. Hoping to take it off
when I go back.

EINSTEIN: I'm going to get a new suit. When I present my paper,
I'd like to be wearing a new suit.

PICASSO: I wonder what I'll be wearing when I paint it?

VISITOR: I'd like something white with a big belt. (*Then:*) Did you
see that?

EINSTEIN: Shooting star. They hit the atmosphere and burn white.

PICASSO: I'd like to leave a long trail. A long string of fire.

EINSTEIN: From horizon to horizon.

VISITOR: Whoosh!

PICASSO: So bright that when you look away, you can still see it against your eyes.

EINSTEIN: I would like that . . . a retention of vision.

PICASSO: I would like that too. Into my eighties. A retention of vision.

VISITOR: I would like to have it too, although I don't know what you're talking about.

PICASSO: I hope I don't die young.

EINSTEIN: Me too.
       (*The* VISITOR *gulps.*)

PICASSO: Are you dead?

VISITOR: Pretty much.

EINSTEIN: How is it?

VISITOR: Overrated.

PICASSO: All those stars. It's a miracle.

EINSTEIN: No, not a miracle; that's just the way it is. A miracle would be if, for example, the stars rearranged themselves and spelled out our names across the heavens.
       (*The three watch, agog.*)

PICASSO: My God!

EINSTEIN: It's a miracle . . .

VISITOR: Just like Vegas.

PICASSO: There's my name.

EINSTEIN: There's mine, spelled right too.

PICASSO (*to the* VISITOR): Don't see yours though.

VISITOR: Oh yeah, it's there. Right above both of yours and three times as big.

PICASSO: Oh yeah.

EINSTEIN: Humph.

VISITOR: Get used to it, gentlemen, 'cause that's the way it works. (*Pause.*)

PICASSO: I want to have the time to make enough things.

EINSTEIN: That's what we do best, make things.

PICASSO: I want to leave the world littered with beauty.

EINSTEIN: I want to make Newton's apple leap back into the tree.

VISITOR: I want to come at them through the radio and break their hearts.

PICASSO: I want them to see the thousand years of tenderness in a woman combing her hair.

EINSTEIN: I want an idea to take them at light speed to the edge of the universe.

VISITOR: I want them not to be lonesome tonight.

PICASSO: Hey, I think we should toast.

EINSTEIN: Got one?

PICASSO: Got a good one.

VISITOR: Sure.

SAGOT: Let's.

FREDDY: I'll pour.

GASTON: I'll drink.
    (GERMAINE *pours several drinks, distributes in silence.*)

PICASSO: I want to toast the twentieth century . . .

GASTON: Why the twentieth century?

VISITOR: Heck, ah know why.

FREDDY: Why?

VISITOR: 'Cause this century, the accomplishments of artists and
    scientists outshone the accomplishments of politicians and
    governments.
    (*Everyone pauses.*)

GASTON: We shall see.

VISITOR: You can take that to the bank.

FREDDY: I know what he means.

GASTON: You always know what everybody means. What exactly does he mean, Freddy?

FREDDY: Simple. He means that in the twentieth century, no political movement will be as glorious as the movement of the line across the paper (*points to* PICASSO), the note across the staff (*indicates the* VISITOR), or the idea across the mind (*indicates* EINSTEIN).

GERMAINE (*to* PICASSO): See what I mean?

FREDDY: I do what I can. I'll start the toast. You all are pretty good rhymers . . . (*He steps forward, swings his arm like a pendulum.*) The pendulum swings to the left . . .
(FREDDY *signals to the* COUNTESS.)

COUNTESS (*shrugs*): The pendulum swings to the right.
(*The* COUNTESS *hands it over to* GASTON.)

GASTON: The past was driven by horses . . .
(*Sounds of agreement from the others.*)

EINSTEIN: The future is driven by light.
(*They all give a responsive "yeah." It falls to* SCHMENDIMAN.)

SCHMENDIMAN: Coconuts . . .
(SCHMENDIMAN *can't think of anything.* FREDDY *steps in.*)

FREDDY: The mistakes of the past are over . . .
(*More "yeahs."*)

PICASSO: The Modern waits to be met . . .
(*More enthusiasm.*)

SCHMENDIMAN (*steps forward*): The pelican's a funny . . .
(*Again,* SCHMENDIMAN *can't think of anything. He sits down.*)

SAGOT: Say good-bye to the age of indifference . . .
  (*They respond with more "hear, hears."* SAGOT *hands it over to the* VISITOR.)

VISITOR: And say hello . . . (*everybody anticipates*) . . . to the age . . .
  (*More anticipation. They all start to toast enthusiastically.*) . . .
  of regret.

(*On "regret," they stop short and stare at the* VISITOR. *Momentary deflation. Then:*)

PICASSO: To the twentieth century!

EINSTEIN: To the twentieth century!

EVERYBODY: The twentieth century!
  (*The lights start to dim or curtain starts to drop.*)

VISITOR (*eyes the lights*): Isn't it amazing how the play fit exactly between the time that the lights came up and the lights went down? (*or: "the curtain went up and the curtain went down?"*)

THE END

The Zig-Zag Woman

The Zig-Zag Woman was originally presented in workshop by the New York Stage and Film Company and the Powerhouse Theater in association with RJK Productions. The cast included:

Rob Campbell
Bill Irwin
Frank Raiter
Kimberly Williams

Director: *Barry Edelstein*
Stage Manager: *Sandi Johnson*

The Zig-Zag Woman's original New York production was by the New York Shakespeare Festival, George C. Wolfe, Producer, with the following cast:

The Zig-Zag Woman: *Amelia Campbell*
Older Man: *Nesbitt Blaisdell*
Middle Man: *Don McManus*
Young Man: *Kevin Isola*

Director: *Barry Edelstein*
Scenic Designer: *Thomas Lynch*
Lighting Designer: *Donald Holder*
Costume Designer: *Laura Cunningham*
Sound Designer: *Red Ramona*
Production Stage Manager: *James Latus*

The curtain opens on a café set. Upstage center is a woman inside the magic effect The Zig-Zag Woman. It's as though a woman's head, arms, legs, and torso have been separated from one another.

THE ZIG-ZAG WOMAN: Maybe *now* he'll notice me.
    (*An* OLDER MAN *walks out, with a chair. He sits alongside* THE ZIG-ZAG WOMAN.)

THE ZIG-ZAG WOMAN: What would you like?

OLDER MAN: I'll just have some coffee.

THE ZIG-ZAG WOMAN: Cream or black?

OLDER MAN: Don't care.

THE ZIG-ZAG WOMAN: Here you are, here's your coffee.
    (THE ZIG-ZAG WOMAN *doesn't hand him the coffee; it just appears. A convention.*)

OLDER MAN: Thank you. (*He takes a sip of imaginary coffee. Pause.*) May I pay you a compliment?

THE ZIG-ZAG WOMAN: All right.

OLDER MAN: It's really nice the way your head is separated from your body like that.

THE ZIG-ZAG WOMAN: Thank you.

OLDER MAN: Most women, their heads are *on* their bodies. You don't often see one separated like yours.

THE ZIG-ZAG WOMAN: Well, thank you. (*To audience, pointing and gesturing with her exposed hands.*) You should know this is not the one. (*To* OLDER MAN:) Will there be anything else?

OLDER MAN: Could I ask you one more question?

THE ZIG-ZAG WOMAN: Please.

OLDER MAN: *Why* is your head separated from your body?

THE ZIG-ZAG WOMAN: I'm trying to meet someone.

OLDER MAN: In my day, they used Chanel Number 5. What's the reason for meeting this person.

THE ZIG-ZAG WOMAN: I want to be in love.

OLDER MAN: Ah yes.

THE ZIG-ZAG WOMAN: All day long, I look into strangers' eyes and ask them what they want. I wait for them to ask me what I want, but they never do. I set the plates down in front of them, and for a second, I close my eyes and wait for a touch on the hand that never comes.

OLDER MAN: Just when you think love is dead, it is waiting for you like a crouching panther. But easy takes the step, easy takes the step.

THE ZIG-ZAG WOMAN: Yes.

OLDER MAN: Remember the dawn breaks.

THE ZIG-ZAG WOMAN: The dawn breaks?

OLDER MAN: The dawn breaks everything, including the mood from the night before.

THE ZIG-ZAG WOMAN: I see.

OLDER MAN: Would you like me to slide you back together?

THE ZIG-ZAG WOMAN (*looks offstage to see if anyone is coming*): Maybe just for a minute.
(*The* OLDER MAN *stands up and slides her middle back together.* THE ZIG-ZAG WOMAN *gets out of the box and investigates her stomach.*)

THE ZIG-ZAG WOMAN: That feels better.
(THE ZIG-ZAG WOMAN *sets a candle on each of the tables and lights the candles.*)

OLDER MAN: The things you gals put yourselves through. Now, me? I've been in love with the same woman my whole life. She's gone now, but not a day goes by that I don't think about her.

THE ZIG-ZAG WOMAN: What was she like?

OLDER MAN: Well, she had a laugh that could spin your head around, and a personality as unpredictable as a ricochet. She could write, sing, and draw, and she issued a declaration of independence every time she entered a room. She was smart as a whip yet could sit down intensely with the morning crossword and not get one. She brightened my life in a way I never could for myself. Her hair was practically edible. Joy issued from her eyes and hands and her walk, and she could sit like Buddah and speak to the fourth place in your heart.

THE ZIG-ZAG WOMAN: You must miss her.

OLDER MAN: I do.

THE ZIG-ZAG WOMAN: How long has she been gone?

OLDER MAN: Twenty-three years. (*Pause.*) Divorced me, married an actor. In the beginning of something, its ending is foretold, and we met in an elevator going down. After she left, in my travels I would sit in hotel lobbies expecting her to appear, telling me what a mistake she'd made. I would land at airports, thinking that she got my flight number and would be waiting for me. When I went to a show, I would buy two tickets in case she had found out where I was and quietly joined me, nothing having to be said. I never figured out why she went away, but I did figure out this: love is a promise delivered already broken.

THE ZIG-ZAG WOMAN: I should go back in the box.

OLDER MAN: Here, let me help.
(*The* OLDER MAN *helps her back into the box. While the box is in the closed position, he opens the stomach window and tickles* THE ZIG-ZAG WOMAN. *She laughs.*)

THE ZIG-ZAG WOMAN: Just slide my middle out.
(*The* OLDER MAN *does this.*)

THE ZIG-ZAG WOMAN: Thank you.
(*A second man, the* MIDDLE MAN, *enters. Midthirties, brassy and loud. Texan. He sits.*)

MIDDLE MAN: Oh, hell with it, I'll have a piece of pie.

THE ZIG-ZAG WOMAN (*quickly*): Here you are.

MIDDLE MAN: Today is my anniversary.

THE ZIG-ZAG WOMAN: Mine, too. Two years with nobody. How about you?

MIDDLE MAN: Twelve years. Twelve years with the wifey. She recently cut her hair short. Looks good. Last night I put my head between her legs, and it was still paradise. I hope I didn't offend you.

THE ZIG-ZAG WOMAN (*to audience*): By the way, this is not him either.

MIDDLE MAN: Tough debate. Married or single. Single brings a sadness, but sadness has its own perfection. Marriage brings a misery of a rare kind, the kind that loves company. (*He looks at* THE ZIG-ZAG WOMAN:) You look like a girl in a fix.

THE ZIG-ZAG WOMAN: A bit of one. The four-wall kind.

MIDDLE MAN: What do you mean?

THE ZIG-ZAG WOMAN: The staring-at-four-walls kind.

MIDDLE MAN: Well, you've got to get it together, babe. There's no four walls inside your head. You just get yourself a personality, that's all. You put two women next to each other, one with a personality and one without, you go for the one with the personality every time. Unless the other one is wearing a red dress. But that's the mistake a lotta guys make.

I mean, that red dress comes off. The personality doesn't. So here's what you do: You get yourself one of those self-help books. You know, nine ways to do this, seven ways to do that. You memorize that stuff, tell it to people, and they think you're a genius. They think *you live by it,* but really you're just going home and whacking off to a record, banging your head against a headboard as the TV sends numbing rays to your groin.

THE ZIG-ZAG WOMAN: Have you noticed that I'm ripped apart?

MIDDLE MAN: Oh yeah, but I didn't know if it was some cosmetic surgery or what. You know, the latest thing. Didn't know if I should mention it. At the parties I go to, you could spend all night not mentioning things. At the parties I go to, there's enough hacked-off flesh to create another party somewhere else. Probably a more fun party, since all that flesh would have to be reanimated by some scientist using pig brains, which would create at least *something.* Is this some kind of beauty thing, like a nose ring?

THE ZIG-ZAG WOMAN: This is just a displacement of the heart.

MIDDLE MAN: Ah yes. But that can be beautiful too. (*He opens the stomach window in the Zig-Zag box and tickles her.*) Here, let me be a momentary salve. (*He slides her middle; she gets out of the box.*) Take the first wife. Crazy as a map of London. Her heart was displaced into the next state. Made her attractive. Every night was like drawing to an inside straight: all or nothing. Ecstasy or agony. She shot herself with a twenty-two. Dumb. Took nine days to die. If you're going to shoot yourself, you gotta use something big like a cannon. Otherwise, you could lay around for years on your own bathroom schedule. Anyway, she lay there comatose, then suddenly popped into consciousness and told me this. I

"What I just said is the fundamental end-all, final, not-subject-to-opinion absolute truth, depending on where you're standing."

© Joan Marcus

"Did the flash go off?"
© *Joan Marcus*

"I want to make Newton's apple leap back into the tree."
© *Joan Marcus*

"Look, I meant everything I said that night. I just forgot who I said it to."
© *Joan Marcus*

"I could dream it forever and still not do it, but when the time comes for it to be done, God, I want to be ready for it."

© *Joan Marcus*

"O God in heaven, which is seventeen miles above the Earth, bless this food grown on this Earth that is four thousand three hundred twenty-five years old. Amen."

© *Michal Daniel*

"When he says that he loves me, what does he mean?"
© *Michal Daniel*

"Clotted cream, and oh, just bring me a big bowl of bacon fat."
© *Michal Daniel*

Patter for the Floating Lady

"I would like her to know how it feels to have no attachments."
© Michal Daniel

"Here comes your misery, wrapped in the most
beautiful thing on Earth."

© *Michal Daniel*

The Zig-Zag Woman

"It's really nice the way your head is separated from your body like that."
© Michal Daniel

"Not right now, I'm thinkin' about the Zig-Zag Woman."
© Michal Daniel

mean these were her dying words; she looked me straight in the eye and said, "I would assign every lie a color: yellow when they were innocent, pale blue when they sailed over you like the sky, red because I knew they drew blood. And then there was the black lie. That's the worst of all." She said, "A black lie was when I told you the truth."

THE ZIG-ZAG WOMAN: How can the truth be a lie?

MIDDLE MAN: That's what I asked her, and here's what she said: "I told you the truth not to tell you the truth, but because I knew the truth would hurt you." By the way, this is so typical of her. You didn't get dying words; you got a dying essay. Then I asked her why did she do it, why did she shoot herself, and she said, "The joy of life juts out of me like the Matterhorn, but the pain of life looms over me like Everest." Then she dropped her head down on the pillow dramatically, like she died. I thought she died too, but they told me she actually died three hours later. Not from what you think. Diabetes. They said she could have lived with the bullet in her head. In fact, it was lodged in the right side of her brain, and they said the only consequence was it would probably make her draw better. Drama queen. Am I talkin' too much?

THE ZIG-ZAG WOMAN: More pie?

MIDDLE MAN: Pie. Pie. That reminds me of something. I don't know why. (*He stands, lost in his memory.*) I was eighteen. I was traveling in Italy with my girlfriend. She was seventeen. She was *seventeen*. We had about six months of experience between us. We had no money. I can't remember how we got there. But can you imagine? Eighteen in Italy with nothing but T-shirts and a bag. Not one word of Italian. One watch between us. No tickets, no reservations. A compass. A compass . . . we thought that would be useful. Like we would suddenly be helped if we knew north. It was August like nobody's business. So hot you could fry eggs in the *air.* We decided to sleep in a park next to the Coliseum. Cars all night long. We went to an Italian market and bought a bottle of white wine. Screw top. We drank it; it tasted bad, but we got drunk, drunk in the park. Sleeping bags, love. Love. The night. Eighteen. We saved the bottle, kept it with us, took it back with us. Later we were told it was olive oil. (*A* YOUNG MAN *enters, full of fire.*)

YOUNG MAN: I'll have six cheeseburgers, five Cokes, one Sprite, two shrimp salads, four iced teas, and three bags of fries.

THE ZIG-ZAG WOMAN: To go?
(*The* YOUNG MAN *never looks at* THE ZIG-ZAG WOMAN.)

YOUNG MAN: No, I'll eat it here.

THE ZIG-ZAG WOMAN: Here you are.
(*The food appears.*)

YOUNG MAN: American food. Yes! I just came back from Italy? I was with a girl; she's seventeen. She went to Italy to get a face-lift and abortion. Plus they can do a twelve-step program there in eight steps. She got busted coming back trying to take a gun on the plane. They let me get on 'cause they couldn't link me to her, even though she was staring into my face and screaming my name in the waiting lounge. I got bumped up to first class on the way back, so all in all, it was a pretty good trip. But I did learn this, though: no more girlfriends that I meet on the street. Hey, guess what? I woke up the other day and had a brilliant flash of insight. (*The* YOUNG MAN *finds this amusing, then goes back to eating.*)

OLDER MAN (*after a pause*): Well, what the hell was it?

YOUNG MAN: Sorry?

OLDER MAN: What was the insight?

YOUNG MAN: Oh, well, here goes. I figured this: I'm twenty-one years old.

OLDER MAN: I know what you mean.

MIDDLE MAN: Keep talkin', kid.

YOUNG MAN: And how much could I really know.

OLDER MAN: Very wise.

MIDDLE MAN: A wise old owl at twenty-one.

YOUNG MAN: I figure a lot. I probably know a lot.
(*The* OLDER MAN *and the* MIDDLE MAN *look at each other.*)

OLDER MAN: He doesn't understand.

MIDDLE MAN: No way.

YOUNG MAN: I came up with this: Every emotion is consumed by its opposite. Every ounce of pleasure is balanced by an equal amount of disaster. Generosity breeds contempt; power breeds weakness. Agony leads to a greater appreciation of bliss. You love your friends, they start dying; when your friends start dying, you take more chances with your own life. Every ache you feel makes its inverse more possible. And that is the ecology of joy and pain.

THE ZIG-ZAG WOMAN (*to audience*): You should know that this is him.

MIDDLE MAN (*snaps his fingers*): Her nickname was pie. That's what reminded me of her. Sorry, go ahead.

YOUNG MAN (*stands, goes downstage of the Zig-Zag box*): I'm tryin' to combine the both. The full life. The good with the . . .
(*The* YOUNG MAN *indicates the others to finish his sentence.*)

MIDDLE MAN: Bad.

YOUNG MAN: The dark with the . . .

OLDER MAN: Light.

YOUNG MAN: The yin with the . . .
(*There is a long pause while the* OLDER MAN *and the* MIDDLE MAN *look at each other.*)

OLDER MAN: Good?

YOUNG MAN: The yin with the . . .

MIDDLE MAN: Uh . . . yellow?

YOUNG MAN: The yin . . . with the . . .

OLDER MAN: Hey, you, bub?

YOUNG MAN: The yin with the . . .

THE ZIG-ZAG WOMAN: Yang.
(*The* YOUNG MAN *snaps his fingers and points, but does not look at her.*)

YOUNG MAN: Right-o.

THE ZIG-ZAG WOMAN: What about love?

YOUNG MAN: Love? When I feel myself falling in love, I go buy a boomerang instead. At least with a boomerang, something comes back to you. Unless, of course, she were zig-zagged. If she were zig-zagged, there you go, that would be a girl I could love forever.
(*The* OLDER MAN *and the* MIDDLE MAN *look at* THE ZIG-ZAG WOMAN, *who is out of her box. She and they rush into the box. The* YOUNG MAN *still faces forward but won't look.*)

YOUNG MAN: No middle . . . arm a mile from her torso . . . now we're talkin'. We'd walk down the street side by side by side. We'd live in a little cottage with a fireplace; just her and me and three little zig-zag babies . . .

MIDDLE MAN: Hello?

THE ZIG-ZAG WOMAN: Hello?

OLDER MAN: Hello?

YOUNG MAN: Not right now, I'm thinkin' about the Zig-Zag Woman.

OLDER MAN: What it takes to turn someone's head today.
(*The* OLDER MAN *opens his suitcase and retrieves the Twister: the Twister is a magician's trick where a person's head appears to twist fully around. He walks over to the* YOUNG MAN *and puts it on his head.*)

YOUNG MAN: Excuse me?

OLDER MAN: Excuse *me.*
(*The* OLDER MAN *then twists the Young Man's head around, 360 degrees. The* OLDER MAN *realizes he's twisted it too far and*

moves the Young Man's head around again to 180 degrees. Now the YOUNG MAN *stares directly at* THE ZIG-ZAG WOMAN.)

THE ZIG-ZAG WOMAN: Hi.

YOUNG MAN: Hi. My God, you're coming apart.

THE ZIG-ZAG WOMAN: You're twisted.
(*The* YOUNG MAN *walks toward her—backwards, of course.*)

MIDDLE MAN: My wife has no head. And you know what, she gets around just fine.

OLDER MAN: My wife could eat fire, and I loved her for it.

YOUNG MAN (*walks toward her—backwards, of course*): Would you like to go to a movie?

THE ZIG-ZAG WOMAN: Yes, I would.

YOUNG MAN: How would we do that?

MIDDLE MAN: Here.
(*The* MIDDLE MAN *walks over to the* YOUNG MAN *and untwists his head, leaving the Twister box on him.*)

YOUNG MAN: Man, that was invigorating.
(*The* YOUNG MAN *takes the Woman's zig-zagged hand and starts to push her off the stage, leaving the two other men alone.*)

YOUNG MAN: Want to get a snack first?

THE ZIG-ZAG WOMAN (*as they exit*): I could go for some pretzels.

OLDER MAN: In the beginning of something, its ending is foretold.

MIDDLE MAN: How do you think they will end?

OLDER MAN: That's an easy one.
(*The* OLDER MAN *waves his hand over the candle; there is a small explosion of fire.*)

MIDDLE MAN: Well, good night.
(*The* MIDDLE MAN *exits. The* OLDER MAN *sits a minute, then brings the Middle Man's chair over to his table. He adjusts it, so a second person could join him. He sits carefully back in his own chair, adjusts the second chair again, then hopefully looks offstage toward the door and waits.*)
(*Slow fade to black.*)

Patter for the Floating Lady

Patter for the Floating Lady was first produced by
the New York Stage and Film Company and the Powerhouse
Theater at Vassar in association with RJK Productions.
The cast included:
Bill Irwin
Carrie Preston
Kimberly Williams

Director: *Barry Edelstein*
Stage Manager: *Sandi Johnson*

Patter for the Floating Lady's original New York production
was by the New York Shakespeare Festival, George C. Wolfe,
Producer, with the following cast:
Magician: *Don McManus*
Angie: *Amelia Campbell*
Assistant: *Carol Kane*

Director: *Barry Edelstein*
Scenic Designer: *Thomas Lynch*
Lighting Designer: *Donald Holder*
Costume Designer: *Laura Cunningham*
Sound Designer: *Red Ramona*
Production Stage Manager: *James Latus*

pat•ter *n.* **1.** Glib, rapid speech, as of a magician, a salesperson, or a comedian.

Curtain opens to reveal a stage set with a magic theme. Slow, melodic music plays. The MAGICIAN *enters. He is forty, dressed in magician's clothes.*

MAGICIAN: On my recent trip to India, I traveled in a small village far, far away from civilization. I had heard about an Indian fakir with extraordinary powers who lived in this village. One of his powers was the ability to levitate a woman, to cause her to float in the air with no visible means of support. I happened to see a demonstration of this in person, outdoors, on a hot summer day. This fakir, or mystic, took two bamboo poles and stuck them into the sand. Then, he looked toward his assistant, a very modest woman—modest but, I must say, very beautiful in her plainness—and hypnotized her. She then sat in the lotus position between the two poles, which she lightly touched with her fingers. There was no noise in the crowd who stood motionless in a semicircle around them. Then, slowly, inch by inch, she rose up; she was suspended in the air. The circumstances were so simple, there was no question of trickery. As I stood there watching her float in the hot, desert air, I said to myself, "That's something I'd like to do to Angie." Angie?

(ANGIE *enters. She is probably twenty-five, offbeat looking in her clothes; wears glasses, but that's because she's quietly hip. She's got something, but it's understated. She stands at the side of the stage.*)

MAGICIAN: Angie plays the violin; she has a busy life, and she isn't
     going for this trick very much, you can imagine. . . . (*To*
     ANGIE:) Angie, would you mind changing into your costume
     now?
     (*Annoyed,* ANGIE *exits.*)

MAGICIAN (*checks to make sure she's gone*): You have to understand
     that when I see Angie, I experience a bright yellow flash of
     desire. And I thought if I could give her this, if I could sus-
     pend her in space, this would be my exchange for the nights
     I laid on top of her, she experiencing nothing. This would
     be my gift to her, even if I do it with black velvet and trick-
     ery, she won't mind, since she understands, as I do, that with
     the exception of a few profound and fleeting moments in
     our lives, everything we say is a lie.
     (*The* MAGICIAN *goes offstage and wheels on the floating-lady
     equipment.*)

MAGICIAN: My love for Angie has never moved in the two years
     I've known her. This drove her insane. I tried to bury how
     deeply I felt for her, but I was weak and my eyes betrayed
     me. She told me once that sometimes when she was with
     me, she could feel my happiness drain out of me; it was true,
     since she could destroy me by answering the phone. The
     irony is that she loved me. That's what I couldn't leave alone:
     "How much?" "How much?" I needed the answer con-
     stantly, not just once, not just with her touch in the yard in
     the night with the dog, not in the morning over coffee with
     a look, but during her excursions into her own life, which I
     knew nourished her love for me. Tonight I want to levitate
     her, not for me, but for her. I would like her to know how it
     feels to have no attachments. I would like her to know how
     it feels to have no attachments, yet her freedom is mine. The
     power from my hands holding her suspended, even if only

a few feet above ground. I don't think she wanted to cause me pain. She wanted to speak painful things to me, and I would deflect them; this would be her freedom. If we could have graphed our happiness, its silhouette would have been the image of the Himalayas. Up and down. Zig-zagging with ragged angles. She used to whisper her secrets directly in my ear; I now hear about her from fourth best friends. Tonight I give her this pathetic gift. This is the limit of my imagination, and my only solace is that no poem, no song, no psalm from David himself could have brought her to me. And I know that tonight when she has been levitated four feet closer to the stars, she will walk out the door and not look back. I know this, so please don't feel for me; the pain is mine to play with. Angie?

(ANGIE *enters. This time in a different dress, a sort of fairy–magician's assistant–showbiz thing.* ANGIE *holds her magician's assistant smile and poses for the audience, looks over at him out of the corner of her eye. She stands at the side of the stage; the* MAGICIAN *lights incense and begins to wave his hands to hypnotize her. Music.*)

MAGICIAN: Your eyelids are heavy . . .

ANGIE: Oh, please.

MAGICIAN: They are very, very heavy.

ANGIE: No, they're not.

MAGICIAN: Oh yeah, sleep. Let yourself drift, drift over the memories, our night in the tropics with your skin cool as an orchid. Black sky over us, pinholes of light punching through its canopy, torches around us, the white smear of the Milky Way extending from Pole to Pole and the light touch of alcohol covering us with its thin oil. Let's float over the night we dreamed of loving each other . . . the night we knew we could never be, yet we merged like ghosts, translucent one on another.

(ANGIE *collapses, hypnotized. The* MAGICIAN *catches her, lifts her up, steadies her.*)

MAGICIAN: There were five hundred nights from beginning to end, five hundred sunrises bearing the name "Angie." Five hundred days ago, I met her and caught the scent of the wild rose, the wild rose with an iron stem.

(ANGIE *is hypnotized. The* MAGICIAN *lets her go; she is able to stand on her own. Momentarily, her eyes open; then softly, she begins to speak:*)

ANGIE: I remember you holding me like I was a baby lamb, so safe, like we were suspended in space. Nothing to stop the movement flowing forward. God, it was beautiful, but time ran out.

(*The* MAGICIAN *is at the opposite side of the stage.*)

MAGICIAN (*speaking antiphonally*): Time ran out.

ANGIE: Like the biorhythms of the pyramids.

MAGICIAN: Like the biorhythms of the pyramids.

ANGIE: Measured on the ancient scale.

MAGICIAN: The ancient scale.

ANGIE: A match that was written in code.

MAGICIAN: A mismatch made in heaven.

ANGIE: My love for you should have had no limit.

MAGICIAN: Yes, it should have.

ANGIE: But it didn't.

MAGICIAN: It should have, but it didn't.

ANGIE: It stopped at my fingertips.

MAGICIAN: Mine stopped at Saturn.

ANGIE: Do you have a cigarette?

MAGICIAN: No.

ANGIE: Are you sure?

MAGICIAN: I'm sure.

ANGIE: God, I want a cigarette.

MAGICIAN (*trying to get her back on track*): The ancient scale.

ANGIE: Oh yeah, the ancient scale.

ANGIE (*back in the trance*): Ah . . .

MAGICIAN: The metaphor of the rectangle. Crazy love. Love intensified. Love so singular it had no opposite. Can you remember?

ANGIE: Yes.

MAGICIAN: Angie, would you let me take you back to it?

ANGIE: I'm afraid.

MAGICIAN: Will you go back?

ANGIE: Yes.
   (*The* MAGICIAN *takes* ANGIE *over to the device, sits her on it, and ties two scarves to her wrists, one to the pole. The* MAGICIAN *makes magic gestures.* ANGIE *begins to float upward slowly. Halfway up the poles, she stops.*)

MAGICIAN: Are you there?

ANGIE: Yes.

MAGICIAN: Can you see us?

ANGIE: Yes.

MAGICIAN: Was there anything you loved about me? That you remember?

ANGIE: Oh yes. I loved you. So many things. The safety. The words exchanged. Letters. I would cough and the phone would ring and it would be you asking me if I was all right. You could imitate me and make me laugh. You would buy me a little thing. When I made spaghetti for you, you were so grateful, Pavarotti himself couldn't have made better spaghetti. We were at a restaurant and a woman came up to you, flirting and right there in front of her, you laced your fingers between mine, showing her who you loved. But the most powerful was the tennis shoe. My God, I cried. After our week in the tropics—where we collapsed, ended—a month later, not having spoken, you sent me a tennis shoe. I looked at it for days, not knowing why you sent it. Then one morning, barefoot, not knowing why, I slipped my foot into it. Sand. Grains of sand still in it from seven thousand miles away; each one the size of a memory. I will love you forever for that second. I cried. I cried for us. But when we fell apart, you didn't understand that I would be back. That if you let me have my life, I would be with you forever. Now, I see other people.

MAGICIAN: Don't hurt me, I'll drop you.

ANGIE: Sometimes I give myself to them.

MAGICIAN: I'll drop you . . .

ANGIE: You can't.

MAGICIAN: I can. You're floating under my power.

ANGIE: No, I'm not, I just make you think I am.
    (*A female* ASSISTANT *walks out with a hoop, in another magician's assistant getup. She tosses the hoop to the* MAGICIAN, *then removes one of the poles holding up* ANGIE. *The* MAGICIAN *tries to prevent her, "No!" but he's too late. The* ASSISTANT *has the pole, but* ANGIE *remains aloft. The* MAGICIAN *is amazed. The* ASSISTANT *then passes the hoop around* ANGIE.)

MAGICIAN: Who are you?

ASSISTANT: I'm working for Angie.

MAGICIAN (*bewildered*): How's she floating?

ASSISTANT: Just don't worry about it.

MAGICIAN: Hey, just get the hell out of here.

ASSISTANT: Don't you think you've done enough?

MAGICIAN: Just go. I can handle Angie.

ASSISTANT: And a bulldozer can handle a Tiffany lamp.

MAGICIAN: You're fired!

ASSISTANT (*to audience*): He read her diary. Can you believe it?

MAGICIAN: Well, thank you. Okay, so I read her diary.

ASSISTANT: He picked it up and read it while she was away.

MAGICIAN: She left it out.

ASSISTANT: She left it out in a locked desk.

MAGICIAN: She left the key out.

ASSISTANT: She left the key out in her purse.

MAGICIAN: She left her purse out.

ASSISTANT: Her purse was in her apartment that you had to drive to.

MAGICIAN: She asked for it.

ASSISTANT: Bad.

MAGICIAN: Like I'm supposed to accidentally find a key in her purse to a locked drawer that I know contains her diary and not have my curiosity piqued?

ASSISTANT: Bad.

MAGICIAN: A moment of weakness.

ASSISTANT: More like a lifetime of weakness revealed in a moment.

MAGICIAN: Who are you?!

ASSISTANT (*suddenly quite serious*): I'm the part of Angie you don't like. I'm the part of her that would rather kill you than sleep with you. I'm the one who didn't call you at midnight on New Year's Eve after I told you I would. You moron. I'm the one who could create a distance between us that was so subtle only your subconscious knew it was there. I'm the one who took you in my naked arms, made love to you, needed you, and simultaneously let you know that I was not yours. I'm the one who took your faults and wrapped them around your own throat.

MAGICIAN: After everything I gave her.

ASSISTANT: What you gave her was confinement in the name of continuous and abiding love.
(*Suddenly, Angie's head raises.*)

ASSISTANT: Listen, she wants to say something.
(ANGIE *begins to rise suddenly, upward to the top of the poles. The movement stops.*)

ASSISTANT: Listen. Here comes your misery, wrapped in the most beautiful thing on Earth.

ANGIE: Dream. There is a dream inside me and a corona surrounding me. The dream is of a bright star in eclipse, and its co-

rona shimmers magnetically. You saw it. I love you for seeing it. It drew you to me, into the dream. But I needed time,
and you didn't have time. Everything you said and did, every
touch at night in bed, every act of kindness, every generosity, every loving comment had this sentence attached: Maybe
now she'll love me. And it made you weak. And if I'm not
going to love someone strong, why love at all?

MAGICIAN: Why didn't you tell me?

ANGIE: I needed you to have already known it. You should have
seen that to let you in hurt me, because you wanted the part
of me you cannot have; you wanted the part that no one
should have of another person. (*She is at the zenith.*) And I
will have my dreams remain inside me, for me, and if you
had let them be, they would have been for you too. So now
I wait for a man my own age who will stand before me at
arms' length, and I will hand him unimaginable joy, and he
will not move forward or move back. Then I will hand him
unimaginable pain. And he will stand neither moving forward nor moving back. Then and only then, I will slit myself from here to here (*indicates a vertical line from her neck
to her abdomen*), open my skin, and close him into me.

MAGICIAN: My God.
(ANGIE *descends rapidly. The* ASSISTANT *helps her down and
leaves the stage.*)

ANGIE: I'm gone.
(ANGIE *walks off the stage.*)

MAGICIAN: Angie!
(*She is gone. The* MAGICIAN *contemplates for a moment, then
reaches in the air and produces a cigarette, holding it between
his fingers. He looks back smugly where* ANGIE *exited.*)

MAGICIAN: I see a large, carved face in front of me with tiki lips, something Hawaiian, wearing a crown of leaves, and he speaks these words: Love makes us godlike with this exception: after the Crucifixion, we have to roll away our own stone. (*He takes a puff or pauses.*) And now, is there a woman from the audience who would like to assist me?
(*Blackout.*)

WASP

WASP was originally presented by the Ensemble Studio Theatre, Curt Dempster, Artistic Director, Kevin Confoy, Executive Producer, with the following cast:

Dad: *Jack Gilpin*
Mom: *Cecilia de Wolf*
Sis: *Melinda Hamilton*
Son: *Josh Soboslai*
Female Voice: *Jenny O'Hara*
Premier, Roger: *Richmond Hoxie*

Director: *Curt Dempster*
Assistant Director: *Eileen Myers*
Set Designer: *Kert F. Lundell*
Lighting Designer: *Greg MacPherson*
Costume Designer: *Julie Diyle*
Sound Designer: *Jeffrey M. Taylor*
Stage Manager: *Heather Robinson*
Production Stage Manager: *Gregg Fletcher*

WASP was presented by the New York Stage and Film Company in association with the Weissberger Theater Group, RJK Productions, and the Powerhouse Theater at Vassar, August 3, 1994. The cast included:

Dad: *Peter Frechette*
Mom: *Jane Kaczmarek*
Sis: *Catherine Kellner*
Son: *Rob Campbell*
Female Voice: *C. C. Loveheart*
Premier, Roger: *Frank Raiter*

Director: *Barry Edelstein*
Set Designer: *Christine Jones*
Costume Designer: *Laura Cunningham*
Lighting Designer: *Howard Werner*
Sound Designer: *Darren Clark*
Stage Manager: *Sandi Johnson*

WASP's original New York production was by the New York Shakespeare Festival, George C. Wolfe, Producer, with the following cast:

Dad: *Don McManus*
Mom: *Carol Kane*
Sis: *Amelia Campbell*
Son: *Kevin Isola*
Female Voice: *Peggy Pope*
Premier, Choirmaster, Roger: *Nesbitt Blaisdell*

Director: *Barry Edelstein*
Scenic Designer: *Thomas Lynch*
Lighting Designer: *Donald Holder*
Costume Designer: *Laura Cunningham*
Sound Designer: *Red Ramona*
Production Stage Manager: *James Latus*

Scene 1
WASP

A kitchen in a fifties' house. A dining table is center stage, with four chairs around it. MOM *sets the table in silence. Around the table are* DAD, SON, *and* SIS. MOM *sits.*

DAD: O God in heaven, which is seventeen miles above the Earth, bless this food grown on this Earth that is four thousand three hundred twenty-five years old. Amen.
(*They pantomime eating. We hear loud, amplified, prerecorded chewing sounds.*)

SON: Jim, where's heaven'?

DAD: Son, it's seventeen miles above the Earth. You enter through clouds. Behind the clouds, there are thirteen golden steps leading to a vestibule. Inside the vestibule is Saint Peter. Next to the vestibule are gates twenty-seven feet high. They are solid gold but with an off-center hinge for easy opening.

SON: Then heaven's closer than the moon?

DAD: What do you mean?

SON: Well, according to my science teacher, the moon is 250,000 miles away.

(*There is a moment of silence while they contemplate this.* MOM *bursts into tears.* DAD *stares at* SON *and starts to chew. Sounds of loud chewing for a long time.*)

SON: Jim, if Adam and Eve were the first people on Earth and they had two sons, where did everybody else come from?

DAD: Huh?
(MOM *stares at* SON.)

SON: Well, if there were only two sons, then who did they marry and where did everybody else come from?
(*Another moment of silence.* MOM *bursts into tears.*)

DAD: Do you like your science teacher?

SON: Yeah.

DAD: Well, that's too bad because he's going to have his tongue pierced in hell by a hot poker.
(*The phone rings.* SIS *looks up in anticipation, grips the table.*)

SIS: Oh, my God, it's Jeremy!
(MOM *goes to the wall phone and answers:*)

MOM: Oh, hi, June! . . . (SIS *dies when she realizes it's not for her.*) Uh-huh . . . yeah . . . really? . . . REALLY? Good news! Thanks! Bye. (*She hangs up, then to herself:*) Oh, great! Great news for me!
(MOM *looks at everyone in anticipation. No one asks her anything. She sits back down.*

Sounds of loud chewing.)

SIS: Guess what I learned in home economics?
(*More munching.*)

MOM: I went to a flower show today, and I just thought it was beautiful; they have the most beautiful things there . . . I went with Miriam and she had been before but there was a new exhibit so . . .
(DAD *starts talking louder and over* MOM.)

MOM:	DAD
She wanted to go again and she knows someone there and she got tickets for me so I got in free. Normally it costs three dollars to go in, so I used the money I saved and picked up a nice arrangement . . . (*Mom's dialogue peters out.*	(*loud and over* MOM): Boy, oh boy, when I was in college, I remember we used to wear these skinny little pants and shirts with big collars; boy, we must have looked silly.

The phone rings. SIS *looks at the phone in anticipation.*)

SIS (*frantic*): It's Jeremy, it's got to be!
(MOM *answers it.*)

MOM: Hello? Oh. Jim, it's for you. It's Mr. Carlyle.
(SIS *collapses again.*)

DAD: I'll take it in the living room.
(DAD *exits. Big relax from the family.*)

DAD (*offstage, loud and muffled*): I don't give a damn what they're talking about if they can't meet us halfway then we've got to reconsider the whole arrangement. There's no sense in

doing what we talked about unless we're willing to do it without a contract and I don't want to see the situation turn around unless we want it to turn around . . .
(MOM, SIS, *and* SON *begin to quake, rattling dishes and cutlery.* MOM *starts to clear dishes, shaking her way with cups and saucers to the sink.* DAD *emits a cheery laugh; the family relaxes.*)

SON (*relieved, trying to make conversation*): Where's the dog?

SIS: Yeah, what happened to Coco? I haven't seen her in about two days. And it's not like she comes back at night; the food's always left in the dish.

MOM: She just wouldn't stay off the furniture, so I put her to sleep.
(SIS *stares horrified into space.* DAD *returns, sits.*)

DAD: Where's Grandmom? We haven't heard from her in about a week.
(SIS *and* SON *look horrified at* MOM. MOM *looks guilty, shifts uncomfortably.*)

MOM (*then*): In Europe they eat the salad after the main course, and that's what we're doing tonight.

DAD (*incredulous*): Salad *after* the main course?

SON: Weird.

MOM: Here it is . . .
(MOM *brings out a huge cherry Jell-O ring with fruit bits on it.*)

DAD (*looks into the cherry ring and points to a piece of fruit*): What's that on top?

MOM: Mango.
(SON *stifles a vomit.*)

SIS: Eyew. I don't think I want any salad. May I be excused? I have to go to choir molestation.

MOM: Okay, you run off.

DAD: I'll have a little piece.
(DAD *takes a piece, carefully cutting around and avoiding the mango.* MOM *starts to cut a piece for* SON.)

SON: I don't think I want any either, Mom.
(DAD *glares at him.*)

SON: Okay, just a little piece. (*He bows his head and utters to himself:*) No mango, no mango, no mango . . .
(MOM *carefully cuts him a piece. Son's eyes widen in terror as she gives him the piece with the mango in it. He thinks about it for a second and starts rubbing his forehead rapidly back and forth with his hand. He continues to do this during next dialogue.* MOM *takes out a letter and sets it nervously on the table.*)

DAD: What's that?

MOM (*nervous*): It's a letter from the chamber of commerce.

SON (*finishes rubbing his forehead*): Mom, can I be excused? I feel like I have a temperature.

MOM (*feels his forehead with the back of her hand*): My, oh my, you sure do. You better go straight to bed.
(SON *disappears quickly, not having to eat his mango.*)

MOM (*as he goes*): Do you want to take your salad to your room?
(SON *indicates he has a stomachache too.*)

DAD: What's it about?

MOM: Well, you know our lawn jockey?

DAD: Yeah.

MOM: They want us to paint its face white.

DAD: Why on earth would they want us to do that?

MOM: They feel it's offensive to some of the Negroes in the community.

DAD: That's like saying there never was such a thing as a Negro lawn jockey. It's really a celebration of the great profession of lawn jockeying.

MOM: They think it shows prejudice.

DAD: Well, that's ridiculous. Some of my best friends are Negro. Jerry at work is a Negro, and we work side by side without the slightest problem.

MOM: That's true; he is a Negro. Well, he's a Navajo.

DAD: But times have changed. I'll make a compromise with them. I'll paint the nineteen jockeys on the north side of the driveway white, but I'm leaving the nineteen on the other side of the driveway alone, and I'm not touching the six on the porch.

MOM: That sounds fair. Jim, I have something to discuss with you. Maybe you can help. Lately, I've been having feelings of . . . distance. My heart will start racing, and I feel like I'm going to die. I don't like to leave the house, because when I get to a supermarket, I always start to feel terrified . . .
(SIS, *dressed for choir, enters with the evening paper.*)

SIS: Evening paper's here.
   (SIS *exits.*)

DAD: Thanks, Judy . . . uh, Sandy.
   (SIS *turns away. It says* KATHY *on the back of her choir robe.*

   DAD *takes the paper, spreads it open, covering his face, and starts to read silently.*)

MOM (*continuing*): My mouth gets dry . . . my palms get moist, and I feel like . . . like I'm going to die (*She continues as though nothing is different.*) And when I don't feel that way, I spend most of the day in fear that the feeling is going to come over me. Sometimes I hear things. I don't think I can live like this.

DAD (*from behind paper*): Honey, it's sounds to me like you're having symptoms of fear without knowing what it is you're afraid of. I'm not going to pretend to know how to cure something like that, but I want you to know that I will be beside you while we together figure out how to conquer this thing. I appreciate how difficult your job is around this house. You are deeply loved. I admire you as a person, as well as a wife. I'm interested in what you say and if there's anytime you need me, I will stop everything to help you.

MOM: Oh, my God, Jim.
   (MOM *is moved.* DAD *leans over to kiss her, and although he still holds the newspaper in front of his face, he kisses her through it. It's a tender smooch and he's so moved, he closes his arms around her head, still holding the newspaper. Her head is completely encircled in it. They break.*)

DAD (*still holding newspaper*): Hmmm. You still get me excited. (*He brings down paper.*) Now why don't you pour us a drink, and I'll meet you upstairs?

MOM: Oh! Oh yes . . .

> (DAD *exits.* MOM *goes to the cupboard, removes a cocktail shaker, throws in some ingredients, shakes it. She takes out two glasses, one a tiny shot glass, the other glass tankard size. She pours the drink in the tiny glass, then in the large one. She picks up the two drinks, starts to exit, then walks center.*)

MOM (*to the air*): Voices?

FEMALE VOICE (*offstage*): Yes?

MOM: Hello.

FEMALE VOICE: Hello, Diane.

MOM: Would you visit me if things were different?

FEMALE VOICE: There would be no need.

MOM: Does heaven exist?

FEMALE VOICE: No.

MOM: Does hell exist?

FEMALE VOICE: No.

MOM: Well, that's something anyway. Do things work out in the end?

FEMALE VOICE: No.

MOM: Am I still pretty?

FEMALE VOICE (*pause while she thinks*): Happiness will make you beautiful.

MOM: You've made me feel better. (*She starts to go, then:*) Voices? . . .

FEMALE VOICE: Yes?

MOM: Is there a heartland?

FEMALE VOICE: Yes.

MOM: Could I go there?

FEMALE VOICE: You're in it.

MOM: Oh. Does the human heart exist?

FEMALE VOICE: Listen, you can hear them breaking.

MOM: What is melancholy?

FEMALE VOICE: Wouldn't you love to dance with him in the moonlight?

MOM (*starts to go, then turns back*): Voices, when he says he loves me, what does he mean?
(*Silence. Lights slowly fade.*)

Scene 2
LEPTON

Lights up. Son's room. We hear Mom's sexual cries coming through the wall. She finishes. Immediately, DAD *comes into the room, wearing a robe.*

DAD (*holding a doorknob sign that says* PRIVATE): Private? It's not really private, is it?

SON: No.

DAD: Well, let's not have the yablons. Der fashion rests particularly well. I hop da balloon fer forest waters. Aged well-brood water babies. In der yablons.

SON: Dad, sometimes I don't know what you're talking about.

DAD: Oh yeah, you're too young to understand now, but one day, you'll have response not too fer-well keption.

SON: Jim, do you think I could get a bicycle?

DAD: Sure, you could get a bicycle. How would you pay for it?

SON: Well. I don't know. I was hoping . . .

DAD: You see, Son, a bicycle is a luxury item. You know what a luxury item is?

SON: No.

DAD: A luxury item is a thing that you have that annoys other people that you have it. Like our very green lawn. That's a luxury item. Oh, it could be less green, I suppose; but that's not what it's about. I work on that lawn, maybe more than I should and pour a little bit o' money into it, but it's a luxury item for me, out there to annoy the others. And let's be fair; they have their luxury items that annoy me. On the corner, that mailbox made out of a ship's chain. Now there's no way I wouldn't like that out in front of our house, but I went for the lawn. What I'm getting at is that you have to work for a luxury item. So if you want that bicycle, you're going to have to work for it. Now, I've got a little lot downtown that we've had for several years, and if you wanted to go down there on weekends and after school and, say, put up a building on it, I think we could get you that bicycle.

SON: Gosh.

DAD: Yes, I know, you're pretty excited. It's not easy putting up a building, Son, but these are the ancient traditions, handed down from the peoples of Gondwanaland, who lived on the plains of Golgotha. Based upon the precepts of Hammurabi. Written in cuneiform on the gates of Babylon. Deduced from the cryptograms of the Questioner of the Sphinx and gleaned from the incunabula of Ratdolt. Delivered unto me by the fleet-footed Mercury when the retrograde Mars backed into Gemini, interpreted from the lyrics of "What a Swell Party." Appeared on my living room wall in blood writ there by God himself and incised in the Holy Trowel of the Masons. Son, we don't get to talk that much; in fact, as far as I can remember, we've never talked. But I was wondering several years ago, and unfortunately never really got around to asking you until now, I was wondering, what you plan to do with your life?

SON: Well . . .

DAD: Before you answer, let me just say that I didn't know what I wanted to do with my life until I was twenty-eight. Which is late when you want to be a gymnast, which, by the way, I gave up when I found out it was considered more an art than a sport. But now, your mother and I have seventeen grand in the bank, at today's prices that's like being a millionaire. See, if you've got a dollar and you spend twenty-nine cents on a loaf of bread, you've got seventy-one cents left. But if you've got seventeen grand and you spend twenty-nine cents on a loaf of bread, you've still got seventeen grand. There's a math lesson for you.

SON: All I know is, it's going to be a great life.

DAD: Well, Son, I have no idea what you're talking about, but I want to suggest that you finish school first and go on to college and get a Ph.D. in Phrenology. But let me just say that no matter what in life you choose to do, I will be there to shame you, unless of course you pass the seventeen thousand mark. Then you will be awarded my college Sigma Delta Phuk-a-lucka pin. Good-bye, and I hope to see you around the house.
(DAD *shakes the Son's hand, exits.*)

SON: Okay, Dad, I mean, Jim.
(SON *stays in the room, takes out a purple pendant, which he puts around his neck. He then takes out a small homemade radio with antenna, dials it. We hear glitches and gwarks, then the sound of a solar wind.*)

SON: Premier . . . Premier . . . come in, Premier.
(*A cheesy spaceman,* PREMIER, *walks out on the stage.*)

PREMIER: Yes?

SON: How are things on Lepton?

PREMIER: Three hundred eighty-five degrees Fahrenheit. It rained molten steel. Now that's cold.

SON: Tell me again, okay?

PREMIER: Again?

SON: I need it now.

PREMIER: How long has it been since my first visit?

SON: Ten years.

PREMIER: Ah yes. You were four, and you were granted the Vision.

SON: Yes.

PREMIER: So much is credited to the gene pool these days. But the gene pool is nothing compared to the Vision. It's really what I enjoy doing most. Placing the Vision where it's least expected. Anyway, you need to hear it?

SON: Yes.

PREMIER: All right. Her skin will be rose on white. She will come to you, her face close to yours, her breath on your mouth. She will speak words voicelessly, which you will understand because of the movement of her lips on yours. Her hand will be on the small of your back and her fingers will be blades. Your blood will pool around you. You will receive a transfusion of a clear liquid that has been exactly measured. That liquid will be sadness. And then, whatever her name may be—Carol, Susan, Virginia—then, she will die, and you will mourn her. Her death will be final in all respects but this: she will be alive and with someone else. But time and again, you will walk in, always at the same age you are now, with your arms open, your heart as big as the moon, not antici- pating the total eclipse. They call you a WASP, *but it's women who have the stingers.* However, you will have a gift. A gift so wonderful that it will take you through the days and nights until the end of your life.

SON: I'm getting a gift? What is it?

PREMIER: The desire to work.
(*Fade out.*)

Scene 3
CHOIR

Lights up. Choir practice. SIS, *wearing her choir robe, stands on a riser. A* CHOIRMASTER *faces upstage, conducting the rest of the invisible choir.*

SIS (*singing*): *I SAW THREE SHIPS A-SAILING IN,*
ON CHRISTMAS DAY,
ON CHRISTMAS DAY.

I SAW THREE SHIPS A-SAILING IN,
ON CHRISTMAS DAY IN THE MORNING.

AND ALL THE BELLS ON EARTH SHALL RING,
ON CHRISTMAS DAY,
ON CHRISTMAS DAY.

AND ALL THE BELLS ON EARTH SHALL RING,
ON CHRISTMAS DAY IN THE MORNING.
(*Pause, she waits with the count.*)

ON CHRISTMAS DAY,
ON CHRISTMAS DAY.
(*Waits another count.*)

ON CHRISTMAS DAY IN THE MORNING.
(*Pause.* SIS *waits, then starts to sing on her own. The* CHOIR-MASTER *can't hear this, and he keeps on conducting "Three Ships."*)

SIS: *SHE WAS ONLY SIXTEEN . . .*
ONLY SIXTEEN,
I LOVED HER SO.
(*The* CHOIRMASTER *points at her.*)

SIS: *ON CHRISTMAS DAY IN THE MORNING (pause),*
BUT SHE WAS TOO YOUNG TO FALL IN LOVE,
AND I WAS TOO YOUNG TO KNOW.
SHE WAS ONLY SIXTEEN . . .

All pink and white and fluffy like a marshmallow. So many desirable qualities. She could have been on a poster in black sunglasses and blond hair. Her pretty ears admired by the choirmaster. All this at sixteen, the weight of the years not yet showing. Entering the ball in a beaded dress that weighed so much she could hardly stand up straight. But she did, this tiny girl from the Southland, her pupils made small from the flashbulbs. "ON CHRISTMAS DAY, ON CHRIST-MAS DAY . . ." I love to sing; I wish I could be a castrati. Boys get all the fun.

CHOIRMASTER: Kathryn . . .

SIS: Yes?

CHOIRMASTER: You're not paying attention.

SIS: Sorry . . . "ON CHRISTMAS DAY . . ." I guess pretty pink ears don't count for much. How can I possibly pay attention? How can I possibly focus on this little tune when I am so much more fascinating? Those who pass within the area of my magnetism know what I'm talking about. My power extends not just to the length of my arms, but all around me, like a sphere when I pass, in the hallways, lockers, to those who hear my voice. I am a flame, and I bring myself to the unsuspecting moths. Unnaturally and strangely, the power ceases when I'm home. There, my influence stays within here (*she indicates her head*), all within. It's all silent in the presence of my mother and father and brother. What they don't realize is that one idea from *this* little mind changes the course of rivers. Not to mention families.

CHOIRMASTER: Kathryn!

SIS: Sorry. (*Pause.*) I know from where my salvation will come. I will give birth to the baby Jesus. The baby Jesus brought to you by Kathryn, the near virgin. I will have to buy swaddling clothes. The sweet baby Jesus, the magician. He will wave his hand, and the dishes will wash themselves; and he will wave his other hand, and the water on the dishes will bead up and rise to the heavens in a reverse dish-drying rain. *I* will put them away. And I will sweetly cradle him. People will come to him for miracles, and I will look proudly on. He will grow and become my husband, the true virgin and the near virgin. Both of us perfectly unspoiled, perfectly true. He couldn't work the miracles without me. I would run the minimart and be the inspiration, the wife of Jesus. And at the end of our lives, he would become the baby Jesus again, and I would put him in the swaddling clothes and carry him upward, entering heaven in a beaded dress that weighed so much she could hardly stand up straight. But she did, this tiny girl from the Southland, her pupils made small from the flashbulbs. "ON CHRISTMAS DAY, ON CHRISTMAS DAY. I SAW THREE SHIPS A-SAILING IN, ON CHRISTMAS DAY IN THE MORNING."

CHOIRMASTER: Kathryn, see me after class.

SIS: Finally.
(*Lights down.*)

Scene 4
YE FAITHFUL

*Lights up. Christmas morning around a tree. Several presents
lie under it. A shiny bicycle stands next to it, with a small ribbon around the handlebars.* SON *enters.*

SON: Yeah!
 (DAD *enters in his robe.*)

DAD: Aren't you going to open it?
 (SON *unwraps the ribbon.*)

SON: Great bicycle! Thanks, Jim!

DAD: Well, that was a nice, little seven-story building you put up,
 Son.

SON: Did you really think so?

DAD: Well, you're no Frank Lloyd Wright.
 (SIS *enters.*)

SIS: Oh, Christmas! Goddamn us, every one.
 (SIS *goes over and casually starts tearing open presents.* MOM
 enters, carrying an elaborate Christmas goose on a tray.)

MOM: Good morning!

DAD, SIS, AND SON: Not really hungry . . . I'm full, I had some cereal
 (*etc.*).

MOM (*cheery*): Fine!

DAD: How would all you kids like to take a trip to Israel?
 (*They stare at him.*)

DAD: Well, all that history, going back four thousand three hundred twenty-five years. All the big names: Moses, David, Solomon, Rebecca, Daren the magnificent, Sassafras. See the manger, the palm fronds, go on the rides, see the tablets with the Ten Commandments . . .

SON: Wow!

DAD: Not the originals, of course; those are broken. Since it's Christmas, what if we went through those commandments? Who can name them? Huh?

SON: Thou shalt not kill. Thou shalt not lie . . .

DAD: Right. Numero uno and numero duo. Don't kill, don't lie. Good advice around the home.

MOM: Don't worship false gods?

DAD: Exactly. Now who can tell me what that means?

SON: Uh . . .

MOM: Don't know.
(SIS *shrugs her shoulders.*)

DAD: Well, you know, false gods. Don't worship 'em. What's another?
(*They all think.*)

SON: How about, Thou shalt not commit adultery?
(DAD *goes into a coughing fit.*)

DAD: Next.

SIS: Don't change horses in the middle of the stream.

DAD: Good one, peanut. If you start out as one thing, don't end up another thing. People don't like it.

SON: Everything's comin' up roses?

DAD: Good, that's six.

MOM: Honor thy father and thy mother.
(*The children cough violently.*)

DAD: Good. Well, there you go. Ten commandments.

SIS: How come it's ten?

DAD: Ten is just right. Fourteen, you go, "Enough already." Eight's not enough, make things too easy. But ten, you can't beat ten. That's why he's God. We got ten fingers, ten toes, and through his wisdom, we don't have ten heads. All thought out beforehand. Well, this has been a real fun morning. Oh, by the way, unhappy childhood, happy life. Bye.
(DAD *exits.*

MOM, SIS, *and* SON *wait a beat to see if he's gone. They all begin to speak in upper-class English accents.*)

SON: Is he gone?
(*The children gather round* MOM *and kneel.*)

SON: Mummy, this has been the most wonderful Christmas ever.

MOM: Well, now off you go to write your thank-you notes. When you're done, you bring them down here, and we'll take each note and set it next to each present you received, and we can make sure you've mentioned each gift in the right way.

SIS: I've already written my thank-you notes. I did them last week.

MOM: How could you have written a thank-you note before you knew what the gift was?

SIS: I didn't mention the gift.

MOM: Well, we'll have to do them all over again, won't we?

SIS: Yes, Mummy.
     (DAD *enters. The kids break away from* MOM, *and they all revert to American accents.*)

DAD: Where are my keys? . . .

SON: Over there, Jim.

DAD (*to* SON): Christmas or no Christmas, I want that lawn mowed today.

SON (*American accent*): I don't wanna!

MOM (*American accent, faking anger*): You do as you're told!

SON (*faking*): Oh, Mom!

DAD: Christ! Where are my keys?

SIS (*American accent*): In the drawer, Dad.

DAD (*picking them up*): How could they get there?

MOM: The butler must have put them there.
   (DAD *starts to exit.*)

DAD: What butler?

MOM: I mean, I must have put them there. Did you remember
   your clubs? . . .
   (*But he is gone. The children kneel by* MOM *again and begin
   speaking in English accents.*)

SIS: I have never understood golf.

MOM: Nor I.

SON: Nor I.

MOM: Scottish game, 'tisn't it?

SON: Oh yes, Scottish.

SIS: *Very* Scottish!
   (*They all chuckle.*)

MOM: Oh, Roger!
   (*An English butler,* ROGER, *enters carrying a tea tray.*)

ROGER: Yes'um?

MOM: Oh. Good. Tea. Has he gone?

ROGER (*looks offstage*): Just driving off now, ma'am.

MOM: We're so naughty!

SIS: You know what I'd like, a big bowl of Wheat-a-Bix!

MOM: On Christmas you can have anything you want. Roger, would you be so kind, one bowl of Wheat-a-Bix.

SON: Oh, I'll have a bowl too!

MOM: Well, me too.

ROGER: Three bowls of Wheat-a-Bix. Clotted cream?

MOM: Of course. Clotted cream, and oh, just bring a big bowl of bacon fat.

ROGER: Mango?

SON: Mango? Oh, Mummy, pretty please!

MOM: Oh, you do love your mango. We'll take it in the garden. (*Afterthought.*) By the folly.

ROGER: Yes'um.

MOM: Go along, then.
    (*The children and* ROGER *exit.* MOM *is left alone onstage.*)

MOM (*still speaks with her English accent*): Voices?

FEMALE VOICE (*offstage*): Yes?

MOM (*English accent*): Thank you for these moments.

FEMALE VOICE: Would you like to be Italian?

MOM: Oh no, I'm afraid I would burst. Unless . . .

FEMALE VOICE: Unless what?

MOM (*English accent*): Unless, late at night, when I'm with him, you know, sort of, in bed, well, you know. Maybe just for five minutes.

FEMALE VOICE: You'd like to be Italian for five minutes?

MOM: I was thinking him.

FEMALE VOICE: I see.

MOM: Well, I'll be in the garden by the folly.
    (MOM *starts to go.*)

FEMALE VOICE: One moment. I have an answer to your question.

MOM (*English accent*): Which one?

FEMALE VOICE: When he says he loves me, what does he mean?

MOM (*normal voice*): Please.

FEMALE VOICE: He means, if only, if only. If only he could call to you from across a river bank.

MOM: Like Running Bear.

FEMALE VOICE: Yes, as well as Little White Dove. He would dive into the river, swim to you, and drown. He knows this. He cannot come close. He would drown. He knows this. The water has no value like it does to you; it is only trouble. He does not know the meaning of the water like you do. Standing on the bank, calling to his Little White Dove, with her so small in his vision, he loves her fully. Swimming toward her, his words skipping across to her like flat rocks, he drowns, afraid of what she wants, not knowing what he should be, realizing his love was in the words that he shouted while on the bank and not in the small whispers he carries to hand to her.

MOM: Is it ever possible for them not to drown?

FEMALE VOICE: Oh yes.

MOM: What makes the difference?

FEMALE VOICE: When the attraction is chemical.

MOM: Chemical?

FEMALE VOICE: Oh yes. The taste of the skin to the tongue. The touch of the hand to the neck. The shape of the face on the retina. Oh, this is too hard long distance; let me come down to Earth.
(*The* FEMALE VOICE *appears from offstage, wearing a conservative Chanel suit and holding a handbag.*)

FEMALE VOICE: Can the chemistry of the breath across the lips inhibit the chemistry of bitterness?
(*It doesn't strike* MOM *as unusual that the* FEMALE VOICE *walks into her living room, looks around.*)

MOM: I see. Would you like something?

FEMALE VOICE (*now onstage*): Oh no. I'm just here for a minute . . .

MOM: Tea?

FEMALE VOICE: Well, maybe just a little.

MOM: Cake?

FEMALE VOICE: No, thanks. I'm trying to lose a few pounds. Maybe a small piece. Here, let me help.
(*The* FEMALE VOICE *helps set the table.*)

MOM: You were talking about the chemistry of the breath across the lips inhibiting the chemistry of bitterness.

FEMALE VOICE: Oh yeah, what I'm trying to say is: sex is the kicker. It's there to cloud our judgment. Otherwise *nobody* would pair off. Once I slept with a guy just to get him to quit trying to sleep with me.

MOM: I could never do that.

FEMALE VOICE: You're forty. I'm four thousand three hundred twenty-five.

MOM: Any kids?

FEMALE VOICE: I have a girl eleven hundred and a boy eight hundred thirty-five. The eight-hundred-thirty-five year old is a terror.

MOM: So how did you get to be omniscient?

FEMALE VOICE: I went to class.

MOM: They have a class? What do you study?

FEMALE VOICE: Every teeny-weeny little thing. We memorize it. Every little rock, every blade of grass. Everything about people, about men, about cats, every type of gravy, every possibility, every potentiality, ducks. It's one class where *et cetera* really means "et cetera."

MOM: That must be hard.

FEMALE VOICE: It is one son of a bitch. You know what one of the questions on the final was?

MOM: What?

FEMALE VOICE: Name everything.

MOM: Wow.

FEMALE VOICE: When I read that question, my mind went blank. Which is a terrible thing when you're asked to name everything.

MOM: What happened?

FEMALE VOICE: Oh, you know, you get through it; I got an eighty-four. Eighty and above is omniscient. Well, I better be going . . . prom night pimple in Cleveland . . .

MOM (*stops her, concerned*): So you know everything.

FEMALE VOICE: Somewhat.

MOM: So . . . what would it be like if I left him?

FEMALE VOICE: You won't believe this, but that was one of the questions on the final. Let's see . . . you will live in a small cottage. It will be surrounded by a white fence. In the backyard will be many colored flowers. Inside will be small lace

doilies like your mother's. You will stand outside on the
green lawn, your face up toward the sun; your hands will
be outstretched, palms open; and you will speak these words:
"What have I done, what have I done, what have I done."
(*Slow blackout.*)

Scene 5
THE LOGIC OF THE LIE

The dinner table again, the family of four sitting around. DAD *is in the middle of a golf story; the family feigns enjoyment.*

DAD: Phil tees off, lands midway down the fairway but off to the right. With the three wood, I'm about ten yards shy of him but straight down the middle. I can see the flag damn straight up with a trap off to the right. Phil's gotta fly over the trap. (MOM *and family emit sounds of delighted interest.*) What happens? Phil eight irons it and flies the trap; he's on the green. I full swing my nine and land right in the trap!

SON (*laughs*): Oh man!

SIS: Wow.

MOM (*laughing*): Man, you don't need a nine iron; you need a hoe!

DAD: So now . . . Phil on the back of the green putts and rolls right past the hole, and it keeps going to the edge of the fringe.

SIS (*laughing*): Did he use a eight iron for that too?
     (*The whole family overlaughs.*)

DAD: I pop it out of the trap and . . . (*starts to laugh*) . . . the damn thing . . . (*more laughs*) . . . rolls right up about ten inches from the hole!
     (*More laughter from the others.*)

DAD: Phil three putts, and I drop it in without hardly looking.
     (*Really big response from family.*)

MOM: Oh . . . ha ha ha.
     (MOM *has to drink water and fan herself. The phone rings.* MOM *answers it.*)

SIS: Oh, my God, it's Jerermy!

MOM: Hello? Just a minute. (*To* SIS:) It's Jeremy.

SIS: Tell him I'm not in.

MOM: She's not in right now. (*She hangs up.*) I thought you wanted to talk to him.

SIS (*practically sinister*): He'll call back.
(*The table becomes silent as* DAD *is lost in thought. He hears the sound of the solar wind. Suddenly he stands up, but the rest of the family can't see him.*)

DAD: Voice? (*No answer.*) Voice? (*No answer.*) Voices? Voice? Typical, nothing. Left here on my own, with only the images of Washington, Jefferson, and Lincoln. Hello? Hello? I'm living the lie, I know it. Nothing but the rules of the road, the ethics of the lumberjack, the silence of the forest broken only by the sound of the ax getting the job done, the ax never complaining. Truth handed down through the pages of *Redbook* and the *Saturday Evening Post*. Becoming leader and hero, onward and stronger to a better life. I know my feelings cannot tolerate illumination under the hard light, but when seen by the flickering light of a campfire surrounded by the covered wagons heading west, I am a god that walks on Earth. Must be strong, must be strong, and in my silence, I am never wrong. The greater the silence, the greater the strength. And therein is the logic of the lie.

MOM: Butter?
(MOM *passes the butter to* SON.)

DAD (*looks back at* MOM): Her. Once, with one hand I held her wrists behind her back and kissed her. Once, I entered her like Caesar into Rome. Once, I drank her blood. I would repeat her name in my head; it swam across my vision to exhaustion. I saw it flying toward me and flapping with wings. I exploded it with the letters flying off in all directions. I inverted it; I anagrammed it. Every word she spoke destroyed or created me. She was the tornado, and I was the barn. I remember her in a yellow chair, leaning forward, her underwear ankled, delivering to me the angel's kiss. Now I stand at the foot of her bed and watch her sleep, and silently ask the question "Who are you?" but the question only echoes back upon myself. Oh, I know what she goes through. She aches with desire. She reaches out for nothing, and nothing comes back. She is bound by walls of feeling. They surround me too, but I must reach through the walls and *provide*. There is no providing on a lingering summer's walk; there is no providing in a caress. I have been to the place she wants me to go. (*Bitterly.*) I have seen how the king of feelings, the great god Romance seats us in his giant hand and thrusts us upward and slowly turns us under the sky. But it is given to us only for minutes, and we spend the rest of our lives paying for those few moments. Love moves through three stages: attraction, desire, need. The third stage is the place I cannot go.

SON: Jim, can I be excused?

DAD: Finish your meal. (*Back to his soliloquy.*) If I can't be excused, why should he? The denial of my affection will make him strong like me. I would love to feel the emotions I have heard so much about, but I may as well try to reassemble a dandelion. (*He snaps out of it and speaks to the family, back to his vigorous delivery.*) Ninth hole, dog-leg left, can't see the pin. (*The family reacts with oohs and ahs. He turns, walks back to the table.*) I decided to go over the trees, but I hit a bad shot, and it goes straight down the middle of the fairway. I

don't say a word! Phil (*starts chuckling*) . . . just slow turns
and stares at me with this look! . . .
(*The others laugh. The sound of munching resumes as they fall
silent.*)

(*Slow fade out.*)